CHASING MY FATHER

Dylan Cramer

ISBN: 978-1-9990512-4-2

Publisher: Dylan Cramer (dcaltosax@gmail.com)
Publishing Assistant: Joy Ross
Photo Assistant: Kat Rono
Cover Design: Riley Cramer

For anyone who's been lost
and tried to find their way back

Praise For The Book

"Dylan, I finished your book. It's quite heartbreaking reading through the events of your life. It's so inspiring how you persisted and pushed through everything. While reading, I took time to think of the people I love and was reminded that I have to cherish every moment with them. Thanks for sharing your story with everyone."

~ Ian C

"Beautifully written, but a harrowing read."

~ David S

"I've just finished *Chasing My Father*, and it is difficult to express how I feel in words. What I can say is that I'm truly moved. As I neared the end of your work, it left me with a profound sense of melancholy, hope, and overall, a mess of jumbled feelings that resist being put into words or quantified. I honestly feel like a changed person in some ways. Reading your story gives me hope since I figure that if you can get to where you are today despite all of the shit you've been through, anybody can.

I'm so glad you decided to put all this into words. The part near the end about love especially resonated with me. Even as I write this, I feel reluctant because, like most other people, I'm too hung up over the word "love." However, I think it's important to be honest, so I will say this: I love you as a mentor, a teacher, a friend. You've touched my life in an unquantifiable way over the past five years, and I'm extremely grateful for that."

~ Matt J

"I couldn't put your book down – You made me laugh and cry at the same time."

~ **Gayle B**

"Okay, my friend, I remain steadfast in my belief that your book should be a movie. You have led an eventful, sometimes heartrending and unusual life. What you endured while living in your family's commune educated me about an era that I'd previously romanticized. How you dealt with the suicides of three loved ones and still managed to pursue your youthful dreams astounds me.

During this time of world upheaval, your writing is truly refreshing and inspiring. You have brilliantly conveyed the significance of love and how accepting and respecting others is paramount to a harmonious world. Readers will greatly benefit from your profound wisdom."

~**Joy R**

"Reading your book changed my life in some ways I can't find the words to describe, especially the part about love. Thank you."

~ **Mudit J**

"Powerful stuff – I don't know how you made it through all that."

~ **Fred C**

Contents

INTRODUCTION

I'm lying in the hospital bed, freaking out. The nurses hover over me, looking even more worried than I am. I'm 63 and haven't been in a hospital for over 55 years. They tell me my blood pressure is through the roof and that my pulse is practically non-existent. I've got a "heart blockage" and on high alert for a heart attack. Too many Heinekens, too much weed. All my fault, of course, all my fault – or is it?

Flat on my back, staring death in the face, everything has suddenly changed. Things unimportant have instantly vanished. I'm scared shitless, afraid to die, and a terror of losing what matters has engulfed me.

But what matters?

What really matters?

We hide the answer to this from ourselves. We plow through life, avoiding, but the truth is always there, beneath the surface, like a slimy bug under a rock that has never been overturned – until now.

For it is only in a crisis that we learn anything, and I am learning now, and quickly – a crash course before I crash.

And what I am learning? That it is not possessions, victories, or accomplishments that carry any weight or value; nor is it needs, regrets, or the unfulfilled. It's *people* – the people I've loved, the people who've been there for me, the people I desperately want to see one more time.

These few souls, amidst the billions that populate this place, are the crux of my existence. For if not them, who? What?

And of these people who have graced my life, there was one that took me to the highest mountain, revealed the brightest, warmest sunshine, and gave me enough love to fill a thousand lifetimes.

That person was my father.

Had I lived for thirteen years, four months and nine days, my life would've been perfect. I would've died the happiest soul on this earth. But my life did not end on that day.

For it to have not is the razor-sharp dagger that carves and slices my heart into pieces every moment since.

Dylan Cramer
January 2022

1

I've been in the hospital for a few hours now wearing a flimsy, ridiculously unflattering blue gown they force you to wear so they can strip away any and all vanity you have, while exposing your private parts for everyone to see; most likely some sort of punishment for being there in the first place. Trapped and their prisoner, I have no choice but to let it all hang out, while memories of my childhood flood through me.

Seven Years Old – Had It All

From the first moment I realized I was here on this spinning, hurtling rock, my heart lived for one person and one person only – my father.

Although he loved my older brother and sister as well, it was clear to everyone that I was his favourite. Something just clicked between the two of us from the get-go; even my mother was jealous of what we had. We did everything together, went everywhere together, and were inseparable. It was as though we lived in a different time zone than everyone else.

From the beginning, my father treated me as an equal and gave me complete independence to do whatever I wanted with my life, without any kind of parental influence or discipline. Because of this, I matured faster than the other kids my age and carried that independent streak with me everywhere I went. Of course, with this freedom I made choices; mostly good ones, but some bad ones as well.

He also instilled an inner confidence in me that made me feel invincible to everything and everyone in the outside world. There was no mountain too high to climb, no challenge too great to take on, and so I did – I took on anything and everything that came my way.

There is a belief in Buddhism that life is like a stick; on the one side there is Buddha who represents good, and on the other side there is Mara who represents evil. They say that one cannot exist without the other, because there are always two sides to a stick and, therefore, two sides to everything. But when I think of my time with my father, I can only remember the Buddha side. I cannot recall a single problem we ever had – not even one. *It was all the Buddha side.*

To have a father like that is what every kid dreams of and every kid deserves. His love surrounded me like the warmest blanket imaginable, and I thrived under his care.

I remember Bukowski talking about how, as a child, he had been regularly beaten by his father (starting from when he was just six years old). For me, it was the opposite. My father abhorred violence, especially towards children. Because of this, he never laid a hand on me or any of us. Once, when I wanted to show off in front of my friends, I pushed my sister off a ledge in our front yard onto some rocks, hurting her badly. My mother wanted to give me a good whoopin', which I deserved, but my father wouldn't let her. Instead, he sent me to my room to "think about it." That was the worst punishment I received from him, ever.

On Sundays, my father would invite his brothers over to "get boiled" and listen to Sinatra records. For some reason, I was the only other person allowed in the room. Perhaps it mattered to him that I experience, as early as possible, the Cramer adoration of Sinatra, but what I most remember about those swingin' sessions was not the stellar music, but how my father made me feel like my presence there was so important to him.

We also went for many walks together. During one that was longer than usual, I suddenly became ill and fell to the ground. My father picked me up and carried me all the way home, without complaint. It may seem like an insignificant thing, but it stuck with me over the years. He was so kind to me, so kind, and he always made me feel like the luckiest kid on the planet. Actually, I *was* the luckiest kid on the planet.

Because of him, my early years were a breeze. We lived in a little community outside of Vancouver called Mary Hill. The only difficulties I had during my time there were two hernia operations and an accident on Mother's Day when I slipped and fell and cut my wrist open. My mother was just taking her first bite of scrambled eggs when she heard my blood-curdling scream from outside. Once at the hospital, because I was terrified of needles, I put up such a fuss that four nurses had to hold me down while another one jammed a needle into my ass. About an hour or so into the operation, I suddenly woke up and saw the doc stitching me up. When he realized I was awake, he freaked out and yelled, "For God's sake, get this kid another shot *now!*"

My second hernia operation coincided with my brother having one at the same time, so we wound up in the hospital together. Beside us was a kid who had a head injury from a car accident. In the middle of the night after our surgeries, my brother suddenly became desperately thirsty. As the hospital was run down and ill-equipped with no way to page the nurse, the three of us were forced to call for help on our own. Two kids with a hernia (which makes it almost impossible to yell), and a kid with a head injury. "One, two, three – NURSE! Okay, one more time... one, two, three – NURSE!" Finally, after endless attempts, a cranky old nurse appeared, and my brother got his apple juice. But the next morning when I woke up and looked over to say hi to the kid, his bed was empty - he'd died during the night. It was my first brush with death, and it left me with a strange, empty feeling.

I fell in love in grade two. Her name was Jennifer Jones. I was completely mad for her, but she had no use for me whatsoever. I remember I got a really bad flu and had to stay home from school for a month. The teacher arranged for all of the kids in my class to send me get-well cards. When they arrived, I hunted through them, looking for Jennifer's, hoping she would send me some sort of secret love message, but hers was as cold as ice. Her lack of interest confused me, so I gave up trying to win her affection.

I experienced racism for the first time that year as well. A family from India rented the house next door to ours. I didn't know anything about them or their culture but was just happy they had a kid my age to hang out with. We became fast friends — I really liked him. Then one day he asked me if I wanted to come over for dinner. I asked my father, and he said it was my decision to make, so I decided to go. I didn't like the food they offered, and their house smelled weird to me, but I found the kid's family to be as nice and as gentle as he was.

A couple of weeks later, unexpectedly and without saying anything, they moved out of town. When I asked my father what happened he said, "Unfortunately they weren't welcome here." Their leaving hit me hard — being so young I couldn't understand it, but the pit in my stomach told me something about it was wrong and for the longest time I couldn't get it out of my mind.

Then, at the end of my grade two year, my father sat us down and told us we were on the move as well — to the big city.

Moving Day

2

The hospital has now moved me to the acute ward, a fancy name for a location where you're most likely to die. After they move you, they scurry like rats to somewhere else, far away – the reason? A simple one – they don't want to be around in case you bite the dust. So you're stuck there on your own, with a couple of geezers nearby who won't stop snoring and farting all night long. Oh my God, get me out of here!

The "big city" was Vancouver, B.C., Canada and the year was 1966. I was eight years old and didn't want to move, but I would've followed my father anywhere, so I didn't raise a fuss. We moved into a small apartment suitable for mice, but I was happy there.

This was a time of revolution in the world. The Vietnam War and the resulting outcry over its injustice, along with the senseless killing of so many young people, gave rise to the hippie/peace movement in the U.S. Thousands of young people migrated to California, and in particular San Francisco, to live an alternative lifestyle of "make love, not war." Peaceful gatherings of thousands began taking place such as the now legendary Woodstock Festival, where upwards of a million young people gathered to hang out, listen to music and celebrate. Free press "underground" newspapers sprang up, most notably The *Berkeley Barb,* where activists and writers voiced opinions not welcomed in the mainstream. Young people started experimenting with drugs and dropped out of society, refusing to follow the previous norms and practices of the traditional ways of the past. It was truly a time of revolution, and it swept over America like a tidal wave, especially amongst its young people.

The movement both confused and infuriated mainstream America and led to many skirmishes between the police and the hippies. Straight people simply could not understand or accept the hippie lifestyle. A huge divide was born as large as the GOP versus the Democrats of today. At that time, you were either straight or a hippie and there was no in-between, period.

To understand my father's role in all of this we must go back a ways. Barry Paul Cramer was born in 1931, one of eight children to a struggling Jewish family. As a young child, it was made clear to him by his own father that he was unwanted. Because of this, my father grew up completely insecure of himself. Although his mother tried to make up for this by doting on him, he lived with the stigma of being unloved his entire young life. And as many people do in this situation, he sublimated this deep insecurity into becoming someone else, going to a place where he could hide from himself and his feelings of rejection. In short, he became an actor.

Luckily for him, he was very good at it, surprisingly so. He was especially good at comedy and would have the family in stitches with his comedic routines. When he graduated from high school he was even voted "most likely to succeed in life" by his peers.

During his grade twelve year, my father decided to pursue acting as a career. It was also during that year that he fell hopelessly in love with the girl of his dreams – Beth Marie Faulkner.

"Betty," as she was known, lived a completely opposite life from my father. Born into a wealthy family, she never suffered or went without, ever. She even had her own horse, which she rode every day. She was a natural beauty with a sparkling personality and a bubbly sense of humour. My father met her at school, fell madly in love with her and began chasing her with everything he had.

At first, Betty didn't take to him, but he wore her down with his humour, wit and persistence. They became a couple and only a year after graduating from high school, announced their engagement. Unfortunately, Betty's father was a staunch anti-Semite and refused to allow Betty to marry a Jew, threatening to disinherit her if she did. Unfazed by her father's threats, however, Betty stood her ground and on June 1st, 1951, my parents got married. Both of them were barely twenty years old. So young – so damn young.

In those days, children came early, and it was no different for my family. My older brother arrived in 1952; my sister, two years later; I showed up four years after that. By the time my father was twenty-eight, he was already saddled with three children. For him it was not a recipe for success, although he tried.

Initially, he tried to make it as an actor, but as there was little work in Vancouver, he struggled. Depression set in and he decided to take a boring, non-creative job at a local television station to make ends meet. He put up a brave face, but he wasn't happy and this unhappiness began to eat away at him.

It was also during this time that he started chasing other women. A local jazz/poetry club opened up in town called "The Cellar" and my

My Parents – Happy

father became an integral part of it. He produced and directed most of the plays there and often acted as the emcee as well. Many famous jazz musicians from the U.S. were featured there and the club became a very popular late-night hangout. My father would work his straight job during the day, catch a quick nap at home and then head to the club for the remainder of the evening. Being away from my mother and the family led him astray and into the arms of many other women. My sister told me years later that my mother knew about these indiscretions, but looked the other way, even though it pissed her off.

This lifestyle went on for a couple of years until my father had an epiphany – one that would change his life and all of ours.

3

It's late at night now and I want to bolt from the hospital and go home. The worst part is my pad is so close – only three blocks away. How many fucking times have I driven past here and paid no attention? How many times have I taken my life and liberty for granted? Too many times, but now, all I want is that freedom and liberty back. A hospital stay is like prison – you don't get out until they let you out. And so, I lay here and suffer, pissed off, scared, alone, helpless, with only my thoughts to keep me company – and then, suddenly, more recollections surface and I drown in them.

My first year in the big city, I took to it like a fish to water. School was only a couple of blocks from where I lived, and I loved it. I was an eager student and a good one. On my first report card, I got straight A stars (the highest mark possible) and one X, which was the worst mark possible (in writing). It turns out that in the big city they taught writing in grade two, but where I had come from, they didn't teach it until grade three, so I missed out on the training, hence the "X." When I went home to show my father my report card, he burst into laughter and said, "An X? I'm proud of you!" and gave me a huge hug. Most fathers would've lost it on their kid and punished them, but not my father. He was so supportive of me and gave me so much confidence, even when I failed. Without a doubt, that "X" wound up being the most cherished mark I ever received in all my years of schooling as it provided another example of how beautiful my father was to me.

Around this time, I also started getting a weekly allowance. In those days, ten cents could buy you a chocolate bar or a bag of chips, so most kids got twenty or twenty-five cents, but my father gave me a dollar, which obviously pleased me to no end.

But the big payoff for me was not the money – no, no, no. It was what occurred *after* he gave me my allowance – he would take me into his arms, give me the biggest, warmest hug imaginable, and say, "Here's a dollar for being YOU."

I cannot tell you with even the most magical, descriptive words available how that hug and those words made me feel, except to say that since then, *I have chased that feeling my entire life.* It was a feeling of complete belonging, of total love, of safety, of protection, of absolute caring. This simple physical exchange, this elegant moment between us with but a few words uttered, was as deep and intense as it is possible to be, and Chaplinesque in its beauty and simplicity. Without a doubt its effect on me was enormous and taught me what love, *real love,* was made of.

The Two Troublemakers

4

It's morning now. Somehow, I made it through the night in one piece. There's a shift change, and the new nurse is a total jerk. He's rude, disinterested and condescending. If I could, I'd get up and kick his ass from here to Katmandu. Most likely, one of these days it'll be his turn to meet someone like himself, the poor sod.

Before I get back to my father and his revolution, there is one more event that happened to me in my grade three year that I feel compelled to share. For the second time in my young life, I fell in love.

Theresa Fox was an angel – otherworldly in her radiant beauty. She had black hair, flawless olive skin and deep brown eyes. From the moment I saw her I was caught, trapped in her web of indescribable magnetism, helplessly so.

I remember the first time I talked to her – I was terrified beyond belief. We were in the same class together, so I waited until recess, summoned up all my courage and approached her. With my heart in my throat, I said, "Hi, I'm Dylan." She looked at me with her mesmerizing, illuminating eyes, smiled and replied softly, "I'm Theresa, but *you* can call me Tessa."

And so, our love was born.

I have never understood why I was so attracted to girls at such an early age, but I was. Perhaps it was my father's influence and how confident he made me feel, so confident that I was able to relax and appreciate a girl and to not be afraid to express that appreciation. But whatever it was, one thing was certain - I was mad for Tessa. What drove me especially crazy about her was her raspy, sensual voice, which sounded somewhat like a cello mixed with a saxophone, and her desire to keep the love we shared between us a secret, *our secret.*

We hid behind trees during lunch and after school and held hands. We talked quietly of our dreams. We shared kisses on the cheek. When my lips would touch her skin my entire body would shiver with passion, but being so young, I had no idea what to do. But what I do know, without a doubt, is that the love we shared was as strong as any I've felt since.

Miraculously, we caught an incredible piece of luck near the end of the school year. A new program was being created for children who constantly finished their assignments ahead of the others. The idea was to put these particular students in a special class where they could work at their own pace. It was called "The Major Works Program." When my father heard about it, he said, "I wish they would call it The Major Fun Program."

Grade three children from all over the city were chosen to attend this experimental class in grade four, to be held at an elementary school some distance from mine. Amazingly, two students from my class were chosen to participate – Tessa and me!

I can still remember the moment I found out. My teacher told me to go outside the classroom and wait for the principal because he wanted to "talk to me about something." Terrified, thinking I was in trouble, I waited anxiously for his arrival. Suddenly, I heard his footsteps approaching, methodical in their rhythm, getting louder and louder until he stopped in front of me. Too afraid to make eye contact, I instead stared at his polished black shoes, fearing the worst, my heart pounding in my chest.

After a moment of tense silence, he suddenly bellowed, "Do you want to go to a school where you can work at your own pace?"

Instantly, I answered, "Yes."

Without saying another word, he turned around and marched away, and as the sound of his footsteps diminished, my heartbeat slowly returned to normal.

A few weeks later there was a meeting for all of the parents of the children chosen for the program. Ironically, the only parents who brought their children with them were my father and Tessa's mother. Banished from the meeting, we went outside to the courtyard, where we played hopscotch together. I can still remember how exciting it felt to be alone with her as we silently danced on those patterned squares. Little did I know that our love was about to be taken away from us only a short time later.

5

It's lunchtime and I haven't had a thing to eat for hours – all they will give me is water, water and more water, which reminds me of the W.C. Fields line, "I wouldn't drink water – fish fuck in it." Finally, the cardiologist shows up and after taking one look at me, he frowns and remarks: "My God, you're so young! Most people in this situation are so much older than you!" Great, thanks a lot doc, I think to myself. Your bedside manner is so charming – not. Then he informs me that I have two choices: go home and risk having a heart attack that could cost me my life or stay in the hospital, go under the knife, and have a pacemaker installed. Bloody hell!

That first summer in Vancouver in 1967, something changed in my father. Fed up and needing time alone to figure things out, he decided to send us all away for a while so he could think things through, and take a long, hard look in the mirror at his life and times.

I don't know exactly what transpired in my father's mind during that time, but I do know that he found a solution to his unhappiness and that it excited him to no end. In Lajos Egri's brilliant book about human character *The Art of Dramatic Writing*, he wrote, "In order to fully understand a character, you must trace his motivation to its source." My father's "source" came from being unwanted and rejected by his father, plain and simple. Feeling trapped in married life and the straight world, the peace movement offered a way out for him and a place to help people, especially young people, who at that time suffered continuous, unnecessary harassment from the police. It also provided a way for him to feel that he mattered, truly mattered, something he had been chasing all his life.

And so, upon our return from our sojourns, my father told us we were on the move once again, this time into a house just a few blocks away. But that was not all he had to say. He then dropped the bombshell of all bombshells – that he was quitting his job, dropping out of society, and starting a commune. None of us had a clue what he meant by "dropping out" or what a commune was, but it sure as hell didn't take us very long to find out.

A commune is defined as "a group of people living together and sharing possessions and responsibilities." Ideally it is just that, a beautiful, fair, equal way of living. However, it quickly became evident that for us it was not going to be beautiful, fair or equal – and once it began, we were thrown into a state of absolute chaos. We went from a family of five to a collective of dozens, all of them strangers. Hippies, vagabonds, U.S. draft dodgers and lost souls wandered in and out of our home (usually close to dinner time, coincidentally), while a few of my father's allies moved in with us on a permanent basis. Sadly, from the moment the commune began, the five of us never spent a single moment of time together again, *ever*.

They say that in life there are those who serve and those who are served; our move to the commune definitely turned us into servers. Our house became a food truck, a hostel and a magnet for every type of person imaginable, ranging from good to downright disgusting. We were open 24 hours a day, 7 days a week, 365 days a year. There were many times when strangers ate my dinner; I was expected to relinquish my food, which resulted in me going to bed hungry many nights. As the commune began to expand and more and more people took advantage of us, the situation got much worse for me. But as I loved and believed in my father with complete and utter devotion, I did everything he asked of me, no questions asked. Blind love is dangerous, and I was definitely blind at that time in my life. I was also just nine years old.

6

Amazingly, I have caught a piece of luck and an operating table has suddenly become available. Before I know it, I'm wheeled into the surgery room at top speed. It's a huge room, almost clean feeling, but not quite. The nurses hover around me, giving me a ton of instructions I can't digest while scaring the crap out of me by saying things like, "It's going to hurt quite a bit when the doctor gives you the freezing." Wait a minute – what did you just say? He's not putting me under? I'm going to be AWAKE while he cuts me open? Fuck this shit – get me outta here! GET ME OUTTA HERE NOW!

In September of 1967, just a month or so after our move to the commune, I made my way to Trafalgar Elementary, grade four and the Major Works Program. Though I had to take four buses a day to get there and back, I dug the independent feeling it gave me and the daily adventures that accompanied my travels.

Once I got to the school, I was immediately subjected to segregation for the first time. Our class was nicknamed "The Major Jerks" by the "normals" who both envied and hated us with a passion. Their rules were as follows: we were not allowed to talk to them, we were not allowed to play with them, and we were not allowed to use any part of the playground they frequented.

Because of this, we did what most would do in this situation: we banded together and became very tight. I took on the role of being the leader of our class and organized all of our activities. We claimed a small part of the playground off the beaten track, did our own thing and stayed as far away from the normals as possible.

By fluke, one of the kids in our class was actually one of the normals himself, having attended Trafalgar the previous year, so he continued to play with his old buddies during recess and lunchtime. When he discovered how good I was at sports, he started working on his friends to let me join them. It took an entire year for them to agree, but they finally did, so I became the first Major Jerk to cross over to their side. That began in my grade five year and to give you a better idea of how unusual this was, not a single other kid from my class was allowed to join in with them until grade seven, two very long years later - assholes.

Because I was loyal to my classmates, I stayed with them during school hours and only played with the normals (along with some stray kids from the neighborhood) on after-school teams. It didn't take me very long to fit in and those teams were not only loaded with incredible talent but were a ton of fun – and we kicked ass. Those years were my happiest and most productive in sports. We made it to the finals on three separate occasions; once in soccer where we lost, and twice in lacrosse, winning both times.

The first lacrosse team I played for provided my second experience with racism. The team contained several players from the Musqueam Indian Reserve, including our coach. Robert Point was one of the kindest, gentlest people I'd ever met. He reminded me a ton of my father, and I took to him immediately. He was soft-spoken, encouraging, and a player's coach. Everybody dug him and we played hard for him.

Unfortunately, whenever our team would go on the road to play other teams in the city, the parents from the other side would shout and hurl racial insults at our Musqueam players. "Kill that dirty Indian!" or "Check that drunk into the boards!" were common obscenities spewed towards my teammates. Because of this, many of the First Nations kids would break down in tears. A true gentleman, Mr. Point wouldn't say anything to these cruel idiots, but I sure as hell wanted to. I couldn't stand watching those kids cry their eyes out – they were all such good, kind people. These completely unwarranted attacks taught me that you cannot judge a book by its cover. *You have to know the person first before you judge them,* a seemingly obvious lesson but one that, oddly, many people have never been taught. Racism is never right, but in this case, when it was directed towards children, it was truly disgusting, and I despised those insensitive people and their vicious, demeaning attacks.

The Team

It was also during my first year at Trafalgar that I ran into a nightmare with Tessa. During the summer, she went through a change in her fashion. She started wearing all black, whether it was a dress, a skirt or a top, along with many necklaces, bracelets, etc. While I thought she looked beautiful, the boys in my class didn't agree and started teasing her relentlessly. As most of them shared the same bus ride home Tessa and I did, they used that public place to insult and ridicule her, calling her things like an ugly witch, a hooker, a slut, and any other derogatory names they could think of.

This presented a conundrum for me. On the one hand, I wanted to defend Tessa from their vicious attacks, but on the other hand, as these were my new classmates that I was trying to bond with, I found myself reluctant to stand up to them and cause any kind of conflict.

And so, I sat on the bus across from Tessa and didn't say a word. For days and days, the boys taunted her and for days and days she looked to me for help, tears streaming down her cheeks. Eventually, I couldn't take it anymore and decided to stand up for her, but when I tried to open my mouth to speak I couldn't; something just paralyzed me and glued my mouth shut.

Just a short time later, Tessa didn't show up to school. Then she didn't come the next day either. When she didn't appear for a third straight day, I asked the teacher if she was sick or something. The teacher answered, "Sorry Dylan, but Theresa's not coming here any longer."

I was devastated. My heart sank and a huge sense of guilt invaded my soul. I felt like it was all my fault and that I had completely let her down. The pain I felt was unbearable. How could I let this happen? How could

I let those idiots hurt her, over and over? How could I just sit there and do nothing?

Losing Tessa wrecked me for a long time. I became withdrawn and felt so alone. Yes, I was only nine years old, but I just couldn't get over losing her. For many years she haunted me, and I found myself wondering if I would ever see her again.

Meanwhile, life in the commune that first year continued on. During those early times, many spirited discussions between my father and his comrades took place. Although I was too young to be able to fully comprehend the nature of these talks, the gist of them regarded the police, civil rights, the underground movement and how to revolutionize, peacefully, the world around us.

By the end of the school year, my father decided we needed to expand our communal living situation, so once again we were on the move; close by, yes, but into a much bigger house, where our life and times would soon explode into a free-for-all none of us saw coming.

7

It's only been a short time since I've been waiting for the doc to show up but as time is relative, it has felt like hours. The waiting is hard, especially when you have no idea what's coming around the corner. So I wait, nervous as hell, worried and frightened, but then, all of a sudden the door swings open and in he comes. Instantly, he makes the room feel as though the clouds have parted to reveal the most vibrant sunshine from heaven imaginable. How does he do this? I suddenly feel safe, warm and completely at peace. He greets me with a voice that is mesmerizing yet calming, as he assures me that everything will be fine, and that he will take complete care of me. HIs demeanor emanates a glowing warmth that is both relaxing and strangely stirring. For God's sake, WHO THE HELL IS THIS GUY?

In 1968, my grade five year started with our move to a bigger house and expanded commune. No longer close to a bus line, I now had to walk to school. Luckily, one of my classmates lived on the way, so we agreed to meet at his place every morning and head to school from there.

The new commune was not an improved version of the old one, to say the least. More and more drifters began frequenting the house and the drug use ramped up dramatically. I was forced to share a room with a stranger who had the last name of Valentine, but I can assure you he was anything but that. A young, angry, confused man in his early twenties, he had a violent temper that would explode on a regular basis. Oftentimes, he hurled pots, pans and other large objects around the room while screaming at the top of his lungs. In short, he scared the crap out of me, and I hated having to share a room with him.

The commune had three floors and was filled with all types of freeloaders and weird types who exhibited strange behaviour on a regular basis. On one occasion, a couple of guys took LSD and then, while high and out of their minds, decided to defecate out of one of the upstairs windows – how lovely. Another time, a girl named Fiona visited the commune accompanied by a very special friend, her pet chimpanzee. The two of them stayed for dinner, and I wound up having to sit beside the hairy beast. For the record, this was not a cute little creature – he was a huge, gross motherfucker. Being just ten years old, I was obviously freaked out at having a naked primate as a dinner guest, terrified that at any moment he might decide to turn on me and attack, but he didn't – he just sat there, silently, eating all the peas on his plate, picking them up one at a time with his massive, pincer-shaped fingers. Then, after a beat, he turned and looked at me and the peas on my plate, which scared the bejesus out of me, so I immediately passed my plate over to him and got the hell out of there. Just another night at the commune!

Meanwhile, my parents started closing their bedroom door and arguing a lot. In my mother's defense, she was thrown into an impossible situation by my father. The transition from straight life to communal was obviously a huge one and exceedingly difficult for her. My mother became the matriarch for all who lived and hung out at the commune, doing the cooking, laundry, etc. It was a tremendous strain on her, and she didn't cope very well as she tried to deal with managing all those weirdos and needy young people, of which there were many.

Another change occurred at that time that influenced my family's dynamic. My father started working for the local underground newspaper of the city, The *Georgia Straight*. His official job title was "business manager" but he also worked as the movie critic for the paper. Because of this, his time at the commune diminished greatly, which left my mother alone to fend for herself. This became the major issue of the conflict between my parents as their arguing became more and more frequent and intense. As I had never heard them attack each other like this before, it confused and upset me. And so, in order to try and cope with this, I did what my father had done years earlier when he was a child – I sublimated. I became completely engrossed in school and sports and stayed as far away, for as long as possible, from home.

The everyday, early morning routine of going to collect my friend for school was an eye-opener, to say the least. His was a straight life – the complete antithesis of mine – a family of four, shirts and ties, eat your breakfast, brush your teeth, grab your lunch, don't forget your schoolbooks. As I was left to my own devices, not being fed, washed, supervised, *anything,* I was forced to take care of myself. While my friend was a slave to his family and their straight ways, I lived a life of complete independence. The counterpoint our two lives offered provided me with tremendous insight and I absorbed this insight thoroughly. While in some ways I was jealous of my friend and his comforts, I also saw how dependent and helpless he was. And another strange, slightly foreboding feeling gave rise in me – the feeling that I was destined to become trapped in-between these two worlds, and that there might not be an escape route available.

8

The doc has given me the freezing and I didn't feel a thing (so take that, nurses). This guy must be a miracle worker or something! Mother Teresa in drag, perhaps? Houdini with a scalpel? I mean, this guy is unbelievable! Now he's ripping my chest open to insert a pacemaker and I still haven't felt a single bit of pain; in fact, I'm enjoying myself! I don't want this to end, ever! This is crazy. As the doc continues to work on me, a sudden idea pops into my head: If I survive this, if I get out of here in one piece, the very first thing I'm gonna do is head down the street totally naked (a la The Terminator), go up to the first person I see and say, "Your clothes – give them to me – NOW." After all, I'll be a cyborg, right? Arnold and me – "Ahnold" and me!

The year was 1969, and as my grade six year began, it would turn out to be another year of change. Along with a few other investors, my father decided to purchase two houses side by side in an extremely rundown part of the city, so we moved yet again. Although this was the first house we had ever owned as a family, it would wind up being the worst living experience imaginable. As the peace movement intensified and grew in its scope, more and more people started pouring into our abode.

Lunch at the Commune

Along with the usual plethora of drifters and hippies, a new type of person started frequenting our place – bikers. Many of these people frightened me, and once again, the drug use increased, highlighted by the steady supply of cocaine the bikers brought with them. Our house became a party house, and the old saying of "sex, drugs, and rock and roll" perfectly described life there. Even my little dog was an addict, hooked on the nicotine from the cigarette butts left lying all over the place. The parties raged on every night – *every night,* which was exceedingly difficult for me to handle as, due to a lack of living space, I was forced to sleep in the basement, underneath the stairs.

I remember the constant partying, trampling of feet, screaming, shouting, along with the loud rock music and how it drove me crazy and made it impossible for me to sleep. On a nightly basis, I would come up the stairs, open the door and yell at the top of my lungs, "TURN IT DOWN!" I can remember one person (and one person only) who would actually do so on occasion, but it wouldn't take long before the music would get turned up again to full blast for the remainder of the evening and into the morning. I had to endure a steady diet of J.J. Cale, Kris Kristofferson, The Rolling Stones and many other rock bands, which left a sour taste in my mouth for that kind of music for decades. Worst of all was the disrespect I felt that was shown towards me, night after night after night, which left me incredibly pissed off, so much so that I couldn't wait for the morning to come so I could get the hell out of there.

Theatre of the Absurd

Added to this nightly torture was a slew of mice that ran through the basement walls. They drove me absolutely insane with the scratching sound their nails made as they performed their nightly gymnastics. When I couldn't stand another second of it, I would punch the wall as hard as I could. Frozen with fear, they would suddenly stop for a few moments, only to start up again. This excruciating torture combined with the never-ending parties upstairs made nights a living hell for me, and I have no idea whatsoever how I was able to get anything accomplished during the day.

It was also at this time that my father gave us the "green light" to do whatever we wanted to with our lives. His motto became, "Your life is your own, and it is what you do with it that matters, not what others think, do, or don't do." Because of this, my brother and sister did what most teenagers would do, given a choice like that – they quit school and became immersed in the commune. As I was a bit younger and loved school, I soldiered on.

By this time, the arguing between my parents had reached a crisis point, so they decided to separate. My father moved out and my mother became the mainstay of the commune. Unfortunately, she became much more than that. She started using a lot of drugs, drank, smoked heavily and became, like all of the other women at the commune (including my sister), available.

A typical night at the commune consisted of partying, fueled by drug and alcohol use, followed by the men choosing whatever woman they felt like getting it on with that particular evening. The women traded places with each other, sharing the men who were around, my mother and sister included.

As a twelve-year-old, this was tough for me to witness. What made it even more difficult was, as I had no money of any kind and had to get bus fare from my mother's purse every morning in order to get to school, I was forced to go into her room, through the white doors, where inside, a horror show awaited me.

Every time I would open the doors, I would see who she had slept with that night. Because the man had sometimes been with my sister as well, it made me sick to my stomach to see him on top of my mother. Most definitely, this visual freak show had a huge impact on my sexual identity for years to come.

There was, however, one tremendous advantage I had during this time. On the rare occasions I would come home right after school, I would observe the women from the commune sitting around the kitchen table, discussing the men from the night before. Because I was so young and no threat to them, they allowed me to be privy to their intimate discussions. The insight I gained from these conversations helped me learn a great deal about women and how they were constantly being used by men. It also helped me develop a soft spot for women that went beyond sexual attraction. However, that insight didn't stop me from being confused and upset by the fact that my mother and sister sometimes fucked the same men.

Meanwhile, my father and I immediately started a new routine in order to keep our love going. Every Tuesday night, without fail, we would go out for dinner, followed by a walk. He even made us walking sticks, and I cherished mine. We didn't spend any of our time together discussing the commune, and I never, ever blamed my father for anything that was going on, as I was still completely caught up in my love and adoration for him. Our Tuesday nights became the most important time in my life, and I couldn't wait to be with him for those few precious moments.

At that time, my father's choice of apparel was anything but traditional. A U.S. Army jacket, black pants and boots were the norm, and combined with his wild black hair and messy beard gave him the appearance of the Argentinian revolutionary Che Guevara. Needless to say, the straights didn't take to his appearance one bit, and I began to notice their disapproving looks, sneers, and heard the comments they made under their breath, things like, "Look at that dirty hippie," or "What a filthy, disgusting person – he should be ashamed of himself."

When we would go out for dinner, oftentimes we would have to wait while the manager was consulted as to whether we would even be allowed to eat there. When we did sit down, the stares and comments bothered me, but I tried not to pay attention, instead focusing on my father. In Christ-like fashion, he never caused a fuss about it, never got angry, never confronted anyone. He just let it happen, let me see it and never said a word. It became yet another powerful lesson he taught me about how people make ignorant, unfair judgements about others based on the way they look, instead of *who they are.*

Another example of this occurred when he would take me with him to the movies. As the movie critic for the underground paper, he would present his press card to the manager of the theatre in order for us to be able to attend a screening of the film for no charge. Upon seeing my father's appearance, the manager would frown, excuse himself and disappear for the longest time. After what seemed like forever, he would eventually reappear and reluctantly allow us in, whereupon the two of us would race past him and into the theatre like a couple of kids suddenly freed from the principal's office.

It was also around this time that my father started introducing me to the homeless. As where he worked was in a rundown part of the city where the homeless frequented, my father would walk the streets with me there, taking me around to meet the street people he knew. There was also a place where people who were struggling could get a bowl of porridge for practically nothing, and we would join them there many times. Just from sitting down beside these people and sharing a meal, my father taught me so much about how to treat people with kindness, regardless of their social position, wealth, or lack of it. From his perspective, I think he identified with the homeless because his father had rejected him as a child. He wanted me to see that these "down and outers" were just people, and as deserving of as much love and respect as anyone else. Because of this, I developed a passion for people who struggled, one that would stay with me my entire life.

A funny moment with my father occurred that year as well. Despite my many sports activities, my father never attended any of my games, which didn't bother me at all because he was always with me in my heart - always. Luckily, one Saturday he was free to come to one of my soccer games, so I was more than excited. None of the kids on the team had ever seen my father before, so when he arrived, his unusual appearance raised a few eyebrows. But as my teammates were loyal to me, they quickly moved past that, and the game began.

Suddenly, in the middle of the contest, a downpour ensued. Our coach, Zale Tanner, a crazy, fun, energetic Hungarian who always wore pointed black shoes (reminiscent of my grade three principal), started getting drenched. My father, who had brought an umbrella along to the match, immediately sprang into action, and started following Mr. Tanner up and down the sidelines, holding the rather large umbrella over Mr. Tanner's head as best as he could. Because Mr. Tanner was so animated and energetic, my father had his work cut out for him as he tried to keep up, but he did his best. I remember looking over at the sideline and seeing my father chasing Mr. Tanner with his umbrella and laughing out loud at the beautiful absurdity of it. It was a wonderful scene for me to experience and only deepened my love and adoration for my father.

9

The operation is over and I'm finally out of captivity. I'm at home, with a huge white bandage on my chest which serves as a battle scar and reminder for what I've just experienced. The feeling of being out of the hospital and free again is unbelievably beautiful, and I am soaking it all in, along with the warm sunshine that is pouring through the upstairs windows. I'm alive! I'm alive! Half-Jews are hard to kill, I guess – hard to kill.

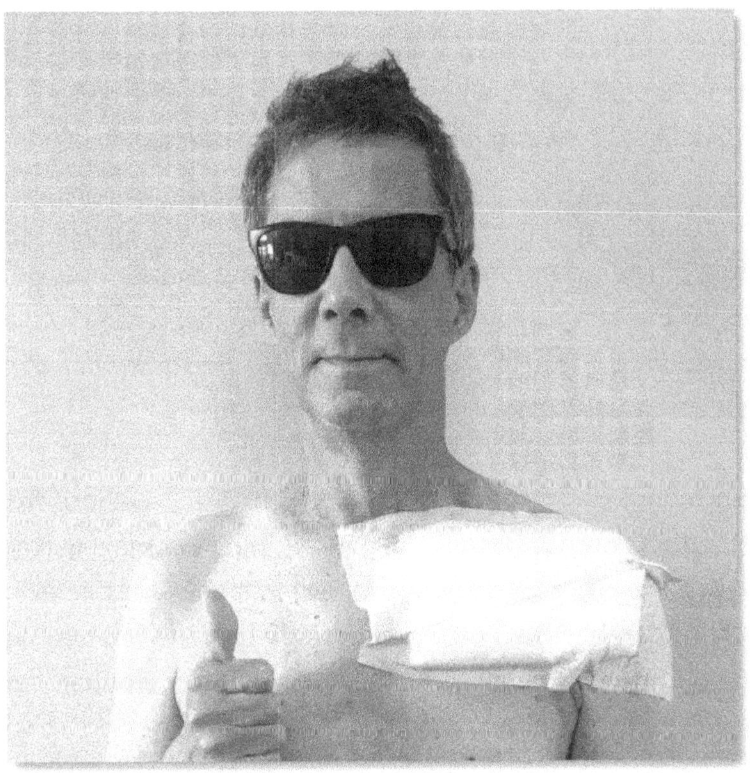

My grade seven year continued to be a massive struggle. The year was 1970, and the commune was now spiralling out of control. A geodesic dome suddenly popped up in-between our two houses, and I didn't have a clue what purpose it served, as I never saw anyone use it, ever. Meanwhile, every type of person imaginable continued frequenting our house while the partying raged on. I started getting fed up with all the freeloaders who would show up, eat whatever food was available, sleep with whatever women they wanted to, and act as though they owned the place. Because of their selfishness, many times when I would open the fridge, it would be empty. As I never had any money, I was forced to hit the streets, scrounging for any food I could find. I discovered a few places where scraps were thrown out and grabbed what I could there. I also arranged to visit a couple of friends after school, and while at their place, ate anything they offered me, not letting on that I hadn't eaten that day. And I found a couple of secure, underground parking lots where I could hide behind a car to get some sleep. Parking lots – warm, private, and oh, so quiet.

Now don't get me wrong – there were some beautiful, kind people who were part of the commune, but they were few and far between. The majority of the people there were users, and their attitude was that they had been wronged in life and therefore, were deserving of getting anything and everything they wanted, at our expense.

This also manifested itself in many of them taking welfare from the government. As they sat around all day, entitled, not making any effort to get a job, they took great delight in taking money for doing nothing. I can still remember the day each month when the welfare cheques would pop through the mail slot. The lazy-ass losers would race to the door like hungry vampires, suddenly gone berserk from the scent of fresh human blood in the vicinity. Their attitude disgusted me, and I started to feel a tremendous amount of resentment towards them.

Unfortunately, I was a welfare child as well. Because of this, I was forced to go to a dentist who received less for treating me than his regular clients and wasn't happy about it. As a way of taking out his frustration, he would purposefully hurt me when I was in his chair. When I would cry out in pain and tell him he was hurting me, he would just say, "I know" and keep going. Needless to say, I grew up terrified of dentists and never forgot his cruelty towards me, cruelty I didn't deserve just because I was poor.

Another small but disgusting issue at the commune was the bathtub. As there was only one bathroom on the main floor, we were expected to share it with all who would frequent our abode. Because most of these people had no respect for anyone except themselves, they would take a bath whenever they felt like it and leave without cleaning it. Because of this, a disgusting ring of their filth would remain for the next person to have to deal with.

Having to wash someone else's filth out of the tub before I could take my own bath made me furious beyond belief. It also reeked of a total lack of respect towards any of us who actually had a conscience or even a shred of dignity. While it is true that in the bigger picture of life, it was only a small annoyance, it did affect me psychologically for years to come. And unfortunately, another side effect began to take root inside of me – hatred, pure hatred towards these people and their selfishness, and there was nothing I could do to stop it.

Stuck in the Madness

School life and sports continued to be my daily escape from all of this. That spring, I had the great fortune to be asked to join the premier lacrosse organization in the city. In actuality, the reason I had been invited was not because they wanted me; they were only interested in a teammate of mine. As we lived close to each other, they brainstormed that by inviting me along, our two families could share the driving responsibilities, as the club was quite a distance from where we lived.

Unfortunately, the lacrosse club had no idea of my living situation, nor did they know that my family didn't have a car or anyone willing to drive me. However, a funny thing happened at the tryouts: while my teammate impressed the club with his abilities (as they had anticipated), *my* talents far exceeded their expectations, so much so that they asked me to be the captain of the team.

I can still remember the conversation I had with the head coach when he took me aside in private to tell me. Coach Jack Crosby was from the straight world – tough, uncompromising and demanding in the extreme. I was afraid of him, as all the kids were. But he was an outstanding coach and really knew his stuff. As long as you did exactly what you were told, you were safe. But if you screwed up or tried to do something your way, there would be hell to pay – he would make sure of that.

After a grueling practice before the season started, he took me aside, stared at me really hard for what seemed like forever, and then asked, "Do you know why I'm making you the captain of this team?"

Surprised by his offer, I replied, "Because I'm the best player?"

Suddenly, his eyeballs practically popped out of his head, his face went beet red, and he seemed to catch on fire as he yelled back, "*NO, GODDAMNIT! BECAUSE YOU'RE THE BEST LEADER! NOW GET OUT THERE AND LEAD, AND WHATEVER YOU DO, DON'T SCREW UP!!*"

And so, I led. Much to the chagrin of my teammate's father, he was forced to pick me up and drop me off to every single practice and game, something he didn't want to do. I can recall the dirty looks he gave me every time I got into his car, and it made me feel unworthy, less of a person, and guilty for not being able to contribute. What made the drives even worse was I also had to listen to him scold and humiliate his son for all the mistakes he had made on the lacrosse floor. His attacks were so belittling that my friend would constantly be in tears in front of me. It was horrible to witness and made me feel so grateful I didn't have a father like that.

Meanwhile, at school, tragedy struck our class. One of my classmates lost his older brother due to a skiing accident. It happened so quickly that it threw all of us for a loop. And this is when the first of many mysterious happenings occurred in and around me, happenings that continue to follow me to this day.

For some inexplicable reason, something inside of me pushed me to represent the class and how we responded to what had happened. Although my classmate was a friend of mine, we weren't super close in any way, yet I felt something within not only pushing me but *demanding* that I take charge and make all of the arrangements, and so I did. I collected money from everyone to buy a card and flowers, secured his home address and arranged for everything to be delivered. It wasn't until a few weeks later that the reason for my actions became crystal clear - dead crystal clear.

10

Hell is not red. There are no pitchforks, raging fires, devils running amuck, underground torture chambers. Hell is brilliant sunshine, blue skies, hope, excitement – and white doors. Those fucking white doors...

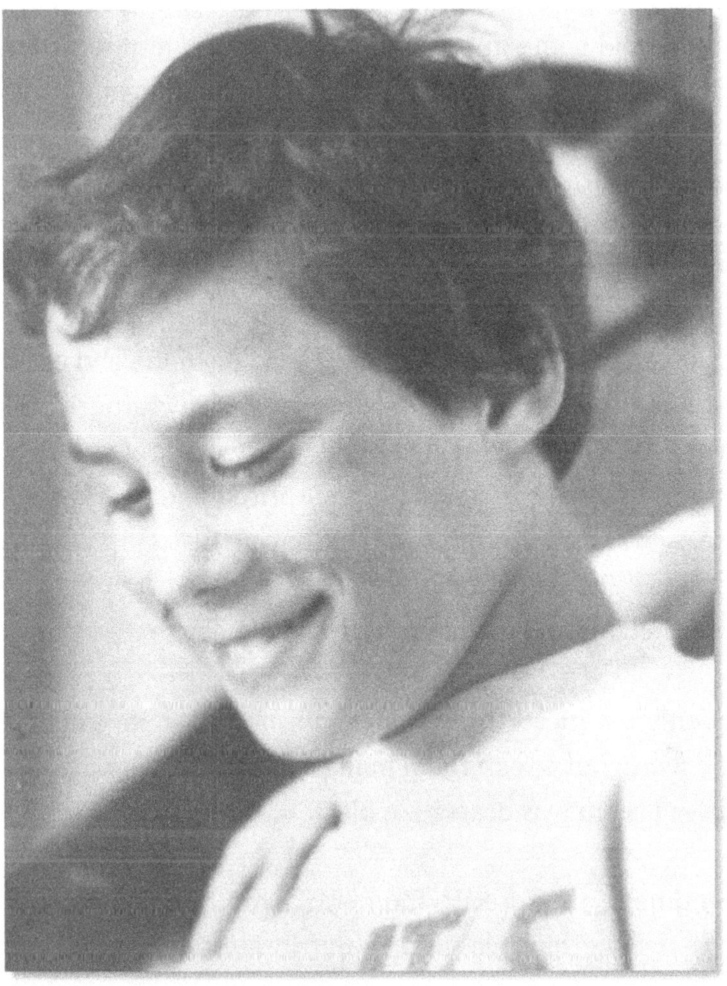

Tuesday, June 1st, 1971, was the most beautiful spring day in Vancouver I had ever seen. The promise of a warm, carefree summer lingered around the corner, while the sunshine and blue skies radiated like diamonds sent from the heavens. Birds happily sang their melodies of the day, chirping up a storm that would've made Brahms stop in his tracks and smile. A gentle breeze was felt, provided by the wind, the hidden ghost of nature, as I raced down the hill in eager anticipation and excitement. Today was Tuesday! I would see my father! And to top it off, it was my parents' twentieth anniversary! Maybe, just maybe, my father would come inside the house, see my mother, they would kiss each other, make up, and we could be a family again!

Such were the dreams that lived inside my heart, as with youthful exuberance all thirteen years, four months and ten days of me burst into the house through the back door.

Once inside, I saw a sight that further fueled my hope and excitement: seated around the kitchen table were many of my father's colleagues from the tv station where he had previously worked. As I had not seen them in quite some time, I was both surprised and overjoyed by their presence, and I went around the table saying hello to each and every one of them. *"They must be here for the party!"* I thought to myself, which only heightened the hopeful fantasy I had created in my mind.

But suddenly, I noticed three things: not one of them said a word to me, *not a word*; not one of them made eye contact with me; and every single one of them was dressed in black.

At that moment, that precise moment, something deep inside of me told me that something was wrong, horribly wrong.

It was then that my aunt took me by the arm and slowly walked me over to the white doors.

The white doors – those fucking white doors – how many times had I opened them before? How many? But this time, everything felt different as I placed my hands on them. This time, they seemed to cry out, to scream at me, *"Don't do it, don't open us up, just run, run, as far away as you can, now! RUN! GET THE FUCK OUT OF HERE!"*

But of course, I didn't. I couldn't. And so, I opened them.

As I drew the doors open, I saw my mother, brother and sister on the bed, all huddled together, crying.

"What's going on?" I asked.

"Your father's dead," my mother blurted out.

"What?"

"BARRY'S DEAD! HE KILLED HIMSELF!" my mother cried, and then all three of them burst into tears and reached out their arms to me.

On the floor beside the bed was an envelope. Something told me to pick it up.

"NO – DON'T LOOK AT THAT!" my mother begged.

I picked up the envelope and took the contents out from inside.

"NO! DON'T!" she pleaded once more.

But I couldn't stop myself. I removed a photograph from the envelope. It was a family picture from when I was very young, taken in my grandfather's backyard. We were all standing together, smiling, in the bright sunshine. My father stood beside me, of course, holding my hand. But the picture had been altered, his image completely blacked out.

When I turned the picture over on its back, it read: "Happy Anniversary, Betty."

At that moment, my mom let out a wail of anguish I was not familiar with. Again, my family reached for me, crying, begging for me to join them.

But instead of doing so, I dropped the picture to the floor, turned my back on them and walked away. After I took my first step, my *very first step*, an inner voice spoke to me – a voice I had never heard before. It said: *"Okay, you're on your own now."*

And so, I became an island unto myself. I shut everything and everyone out of my life. A line crossed with no way back. No way back.

11

It's the morning after. I'm at the lacrosse box, alone, way before most people are up and around. I'm throwing the ball against the boards as hard as I can, over and over, relentlessly. My arms, aching and on fire, beg me to stop, but I don't listen. I keep pounding the ball against the wall. A feeling of total emptiness surrounds me. Such is my new existence, without him.

The death of my father plunged me into isolation and blew my trust system to smithereens, like stepping on a land mine in my heart. Because of this, I retreated from everyone and everything and trusted no one. I avoided my family and the commune like the plague and took to the streets. I lost all of my confidence, all of my strength and everything positive that I formerly had, while a darkness invaded, blacker than black, that spread like wildfire inside me – *deathfire.*

Everyone deals with death differently. Some scream and cry in pain; others seek the support of friends and family; some reach out to therapists or medication. I did none of those things, but instead, followed the instructions the voice had given me. I removed myself from the world, held all of my emotions inside, and spoke to no one. And for the first time in my life, I had a secret – a horrible secret that tortured me, that I carried with me everywhere I went. This secret began to eat away at me, slowly and methodically, and there was nothing I could do to stop it. It forced my emotions to become completely non-existent, sealed off, deleted, while it spread its roots inside of me and grew like a poisonous weed, out of control.

How to move forward? And to where? *Where?*

12

A couple of days after my father's death, I found myself at the commune. Suddenly, there was a knock on the door. As everyone else was either passed out or in bed screwing, I was forced to answer. It was a delivery guy, with the proverbial flowers and card from my classmates— my turn to receive the useless death gift I had prepared for my classmate just a few weeks earlier. While the irony of it was not lost on me, I was not amused. I threw the flowers in the garbage, ripped the card to shreds and got the hell out of there.

As it was approaching the end of the school year, I needed to grab a few of my things, so I reluctantly made an appearance at school. Riding through the park, I suddenly leapt off my bike and impulsively hurled it forward with all of my might. The kids in the vicinity immediately stopped in their tracks to watch as my ten-speed careened off course and crashed to the ground. Some of them laughed, a nervous laugh, while most of them got as far away from me as possible. I paid zero attention to any of them, retrieved my bike and carried on to the classroom.

Once inside, I said nothing to anyone. The tension in the room was uncomfortable and awkward. Then all of a sudden, Cheryl Brooks walked up to me. I had crushed on her for at least the last two years running, but she had never responded, not even once. But today was different, and she came over to me, smiled, and with her cute little lisp said, "Hey, Dylie Bar – nithce to thee you."

For the first time since my father had died, I felt my heart open. Suddenly, I desperately wanted to hold her, be comforted by her, to fall into her arms. But as quickly as my heart opened, it immediately slammed shut. It was a signal, a signal from within, that feelings would no longer be tolerated. This was the new me.

And with that realization, I turned away and walked out, never to return.

13

After a few days of strange calm, the commune resumed its modus operandi as the endless, late-night partying started up once again. My mother and sister picked up right where they left off, while my brother made a new best friend – heroin. Soon after, he fell ill with hepatitis, then jaundice as he almost bit the dust at eighteen years of age. Nice try, broheim…

Meanwhile, I had a lacrosse game to play. It was the playoffs, and the expectations were high. As I could no longer stomach the idea of sitting in my teammate's car, I rode my bike to the game. It was a long way, but at least I was on my own, which is the only place I wanted to be.

I suited up and went through the motions in preparation for the contest. Once the game started, I temporarily lost myself in the action until suddenly a searing, stabbing pain cut through my stomach, causing me to double over in agony. I dropped my stick to the floor and stopped dead in my tracks. Somehow, I made it over to the bench, and once there, received a hate stare from Coach Crosby that would've melted an iceberg in the Arctic.

Later on, something truly frightening occurred. Running down the floor with my teammates, I suddenly saw him – my father. We were walking on the beach with our walking sticks, frolicking and having fun as we had done so many times. As this cherished memory played out in my mind, my father turned to me to speak, but when he opened his mouth, no sound came out. His lips were moving, but no sound. NO SOUND!

As I watched this nightmare unfold, a rush of terror gripped me. The next thing I knew, the ball hit me in the chest, soon to be retrieved by the opposition. Still stunned by what I had just seen, I made my way off the floor as the glare of anger I received from Crosby was off the charts.

After the game, which we lost, Crosby confronted me in the hallway.

"What the hell happened out there today?" he asked.

Unable to answer, I stared at the floor in silence.

"If you ever screw up like that again, you're finished!" he barked and stormed off.

He was a man of few words but knew how to get his point across.

A few days later, my mother took me to the doctor. I don't know why she did, or why I even told her what had happened. Despite her drug and alcohol addictions, she was a very attractive woman, and as soon as the doctor laid eyes on her, he started coming on to her. After flirting with her non-stop for an annoying amount of time, he finally turned to me and delivered his verdict for my predicament: "Quit sports." Then he turned back to my mother and did his best to get a date with her, to no avail.

And so, I quit. I don't know why I listened to that sex-starved quack, but I did. A sign of inner weakness, most likely. I had nothing to fight with and no reason to fight anymore, now that my father was gone.

Quitting sports was a serious blow to my existence. From my earliest days, I had dreamt of being a professional athlete. Everything in my life had been geared towards achieving that goal. Now, all of that was dead, vanished into thin air.

Something that bothered me for years afterwards was why Crosby did nothing when I quit the team. Perhaps if he had come after me and tried to talk me into staying, I might've made it through somehow. But instead, he said and did nothing. This further destroyed my confidence in myself and led me to give up without a fight.

Summer arrived, and with it the realization that grade eight and high school were around the corner, and no one would know me there. The anonymity that would provide was exactly what I wanted and needed – a place to hide from everyone and everything.

14

Though the summer slipped past like a blur, the voice spoke to me again. I didn't know who it was or where it was coming from, but it spoke with authority. It commanded me and for some reason I followed it, without question. "Play music," it ordered. And so, I did – I took up the alto saxophone.

As my grade eight year began, so did my obsession with the alto saxophone. It became my key, my escape from everything and everyone, and I poured myself into perfecting it. Unfortunately, I had no special talents, so my progress was slow, but I kept at it, practicing every day for hours on end.

Now at a new school, I went to great lengths to hide my past. No one knew anything about my living situation or the death of my father. However, the vice principal of the school, Barney O'Brien, somehow recognized that I was damaged and took an interest in me. He offered me a master key to the school (which was unheard of) and told me I could practice my saxophone in any room that was available. He also gave me the green light to stay at school as late as I wanted, which I took advantage of almost every night. Why did he do these things? Why was he so kind to me? *And how could he tell I was a fucked-up mess?*

Along with my unexpected friendship with Mr. O'Brien, I also became close with another person at school – the janitor. Looking as white as a ghost, he was definitely an odd character with his gaunt frame, hollow eyes, disheveled hair, sweat-stained shirt, baggy pants and worn-out shoes. But underneath this bizarre exterior was a kind person, someone I recognized as being out of place in this world, who I could therefore relate to. Of course, the kids mocked and teased him at every opportunity, mostly because of their fear of him. It was another circumstance where judgements were made based on appearance only, and it pissed me off. Oftentimes during school hours, I would visit him in the boiler room, where he spent most of his time. He didn't talk much – mostly grunted and groaned, but a silent recognition and bond developed between us. Two souls, lost, adrift, like two ships passing each other at sea in the night.

Meanwhile, Mr. O'Brien continued to be incredibly kind. He offered me a summer job painting the seminar rooms at the school that paid fifty bucks, money I desperately needed. Unfortunately, while I was there, I witnessed something that resonated with me all too well and crushed my heart once again.

Two or three other kids were also hired to paint the seminar rooms, and one of them was a girl I didn't know. During a break from painting, one of the boys asked her what her father did. She hesitated, and I felt my heart jump into my throat.

There is some sort of strange rite of passage that produces this question between young people – a question I dreaded and avoided answering every time it came my way. Obviously, the girl was avoiding it as well.

When she didn't answer, the boy asked her again. "What does your father do?"

She paused again, but then under her breath she responded, "He works in a grave."

The boy, too stupid to catch on said, "What?"

She answered again, "He works in a grave."

"I don't get it" the boy responded and then as the girl burst into tears, his friend snapped at him and yelled, "You idiot – *he's dead!*"

My heart sank. I knew how hard that must've been for her and that I didn't have the kind of courage she had. I wanted to comfort her, to hold her, but I didn't. I just watched her tears spill all over her, while I couldn't get her answer out of my mind. "*He works in a grave. He works in a grave.*" *FUCK!*

15

Despite the fact that I had quit the lacrosse team and all sports, I still went to the lacrosse box regularly to burn the ball against the wall. This particular morning, it was later than usual, and there were some kids in there, younger than me, goofing around and having fun. Pissed off by their presence, I jumped off my bike and threw it as hard as I could in their direction. As the bike crashed into the ground, the kids scampered out of the box as quickly as possible, leaving it empty for me and me only.

Now in grade nine, my passion for the saxophone continued to increase on a daily basis. Luckily, the band teacher was fantastic, and all the kids dug him. I excelled in band and got top marks in all my other subjects as well. I even became the grade nine president, beating out another very popular kid who had a life of ease I could only dream of having.

Around this time, kids started having house parties. In those days, drinking was the only conduit for getting high, unlike at my house, where everything imaginable was available. Even though I was well-liked and invited, I refused to attend any of those parties. The reasoning was obvious – I had lived in a party for years now and detested them. The idea of going to a party to get wasted disgusted me. Fourteen years old and already burned out – this was my fate.

Actually, I do remember attending one party during high school. I found a pretty girl and sat down beside her to make small talk, and she offered me a beer. However, when she cracked open the bottle with her teeth, her attractiveness suddenly disappeared, and I bolted out of there.

I lost my virginity at the commune that year. It happened with one of the girls who was a regular there, a girl of twenty-two. After I had taken a bath, she asked if she could dry my hair for me. Surprised, I said yes, and so she came to my room. After she started playing with my hair, I suddenly became aroused, and we made love. As I was only fourteen and completely inexperienced, the entire session lasted less than a minute, but I felt tenderness towards her.

After that, I visited her two or three times, and we made love each time. But the next time I went to see her, she stopped me. She said, "I'm sorry, Dylan, but I need more than just sex." Confused, I walked out on her, and our relations ended. I felt somehow that I had done something wrong and kept what had happened between us a secret.

16

By the time I reached sixteen, I had been carrying the secret of my father's suicide inside of me for three torturous years. The secret ate away at me from within; it never left me or stopped tormenting me. I became a liar, an actor, an incredible actor, constantly on the stage, forced to live a double life. Eventually this caught up with me and began to manifest itself in destructive ways. For me, those ways were intense hatred towards the world and horrific acne, both of which further scarred my self-confidence and drove me deeper into myself, away from everyone else and the world at large.

During my grade ten year, I continued to avoid the commune, rarely making an appearance there. An uncle was able to offer me a job cleaning his store, which gave me some much-needed bread that I put to good use. Little did I know at the time, however, that the main reason he was helping me was to use that as leverage to try and get into my mother's pants. This was the same jerk who claimed he had been my father's best friend — really? I'm not sure whether he was successful or not with my mother, but my instincts told me he wasn't, as it didn't take long before my job working for him was unceremoniously terminated.

Shortly afterwards, a cousin of mine introduced me to a saxophone teacher he was taking lessons from. The teacher was fun, energetic and positive. We hit it off immediately and although it was a long bus ride away, I started taking lessons from him.

After a couple of months, he told me he was going to start a band to go on the road and tour Canada. He asked me if I would be interested in being a part of it, and I immediately said yes. This was my ticket out of the commune, and I grabbed the opportunity.

And so, in January of 1975, at age seventeen, I took off on the road, no direction home.

17

Just a few months before I hit the road, I had fallen for a girl from school. She was two years younger than me, and like Tessa, had black hair, gorgeous skin and a smile brighter than sunshine. But unlike my time with Tessa, this time around I was damaged, and so I used this girl, taking advantage of her and her sweet innocence in every way possible. I cheated on her, I manipulated her, I lied to her. Worst of all, the cruel nature of my actions didn't bother me in the least. Evil reigned inside me, as did a total and utter lack of conscience, something I would have to battle all my life.

The road was a welcome escape from the commune. Despite being the only underage person in the band, I was treated as an equal by the other nine guys. The band featured the big band music of the 1940s along with some cool jazz tunes thrown into the mix. We called ourselves "Perdido."

As we made our way across Western Canada over the next few months, it began to become clear that we were not getting paid properly. As my saxophone teacher was the leader, I found it hard to fathom that he would be stealing from the band, but that is exactly what he had been doing. A decision was made to fire him, and I volunteered to take his place.

I relished the opportunity to take charge of the band and truly enjoyed it. I booked the gigs, negotiated our salary and always paid the guys in full and on time. During my time as the leader, we did extremely well and I was able to send $1,500 home to my mother to keep for me for my future education.

A few memories from that year on the road stand out. At a gig I secured for us at a Sheraton Hotel, I became friends with a woman who was a high-end call girl that frequented the club on a nightly basis. She dressed elegantly, was very classy and extremely intelligent, reminiscent of the character Mimi Rogers played in Ridley Scott's classic film *Someone To Watch Over Me*. Because of my experiences with the women from the commune, I connected with her easily and we became fast friends. I looked forward to hanging out with her every night until she had customers to attend to. I developed very strong feelings for her, so strong in fact, that if she had asked me to stay, I would've done so. Something about her just made me feel safe and comfortable, things I hadn't felt in a very long time, which made it extremely difficult for me to say goodbye.

In another city, we did our usual clinic and concert at the local school, and afterwards, partied with several of the female teachers. One thing led to another, and I found myself on the floor of my hotel room making love with one of them. The next morning, with both of us very hungover, she woke up, rolled over and said, "Good morning, Brian." Ugh – life as a musician on the road.

My final gig with the band was in Vancouver, at The Cave, a well-established nightclub now on the decline. Formerly a place where first-rate artists such as Lena Horne and Count Basie performed, it was now home to a slew of "B" artists, and we were hired as the house band to back them up.

After one particular engagement, I went into the office to collect the money for the band. The owner at that time was a tough Italian who was intimidating to most of the people who came in contact with him. However, having dealt with bikers for years at the commune, he didn't scare me one bit.

As he counted out the money for the band, I suddenly realized that he had screwed up. Instead of paying me $2,000 for the week, he had paid me $10,000! Suddenly, I experienced a flashback to when I was living at the commune. Occasionally, my mother, too wasted to function, would ask me to do some grocery shopping, and on one particular occasion, she had given me a hundred-dollar bill to do so (don't ask me where she got the money). In those days, you couldn't go to a grocery store with a bill that large, so I stopped at a local bank to ask for change. After the young teller gathered the bills together, she counted, "Twenty, forty, sixty, eighty, one … twenty, forty, sixty, eighty, two." *She had given me an extra hundred dollars by mistake!*

Being twelve years old and poor, I had never seen this much money before and an inner crisis ensued as to whether to keep the money or not. I decided to keep the money but felt guilty about it, worried that she would get in trouble because of her error.

Now, five years later, I found myself in the same predicament, and although I must confess that I did hesitate for a moment, this time I did the right thing, pushing the money back towards him while yelling, "You idiot! It's TWO thousand, not TEN!"

From that moment on, although I was a minor, whenever I showed up at The Cave, I got the best seat in the house, free food and all the booze

I could drink.

Occasionally, during that year on the road, we found ourselves back home for a brief spell. At one of those stopovers, a major turning point occurred in my life. My best friend from high school, a guitar player, gave me an album of a saxophonist and urged me to listen to him.

The saxophonist was William Mansfield Turner, known to the world as Sonny Criss. As soon as I heard Sonny play, I was mesmerized, but something else happened as well – the voice returned. Again, its order was simple and direct. "Go to him," it commanded. And so, from that moment on, all of my energy and focus became to get to Sonny Criss.

I finished out the year with Perdido and headed home. I had one more semester of high school to complete and then my plan was to head to Los Angeles to find Sonny. I planned to use the $1,500 I had sent home for my trip to LA.

Unfortunately, my mother had other plans for my money, which she blew up her nose to feed her cocaine habit. When I arrived home and asked her for it, she simply didn't answer. I was beyond furious with her for stealing from me. We didn't talk for a long time after that.

Now stuck in Vancouver, broke, I finished off high school and took a job at a local record store. Once again, I started saving up for my journey down south. This time, however, I kept the money hidden from my mother...

After eight months of working, I finally had enough bread to split town, so in late March of 1977, along with a couple of friends, I took off for

SoCal. I was nineteen years old.

18

The night we arrived in Los Angeles was March 27th, 1977. After grabbing a cheap motel room for the evening, we turned on the television to receive the shocking, bizarre news that two Boeing 747s in Tenerife, Spain had crashed into each other, killing 583 people. The worst aviation disaster in history, and a strange way to kickstart our time in LA.

After securing a place to rent in Van Nuys, located in the San Fernando Valley, I immediately headed to the nearest record store to look for Sonny Criss albums. I found him in the jazz section and there it was – Sonny's newest album, *Warm and Sonny*. On the front cover was a nice shot of LA with bright sunshine and palm trees, but when I turned the album over, there was a full shot of Sonny, dressed in a suit, looking mean and nasty, with cigarette smoke billowing out of his nose. The picture scared me, but I forced myself to not let it deter me from my goal, and a few days later, took the plunge and called him.

Unfortunately, Sonny wasn't interested in hearing from me. He was rude, offensive and angry, yelling, "I don't teach!" as he hung up on me. When I phoned him a second time a few days later, he said, "YOU again? I told you I don't teach!" and slammed the phone down yet again. Even though this continued a few more times, I kept calling until one day he suddenly asked, "How long are your fingers, boy?" When I hesitated, he yelled, "Well, short, medium, or long?" When I answered, "Medium, I guess," he said, "Okay, call me back next week."

During our next call, he asked, "How much you wanna pay for lessons, boy?" When I said, "I don't know – twenty?" he suddenly burst out laughing and exclaimed, "You said it, boy – *you said it!*" Shortly thereafter, a lesson was arranged, and my dream was about to come true – I would meet the great Sonny Criss.

The "Warm and Sonny" Shot

19

It takes about six weeks to become infected in "the jungle." First, you get a cold, a cold that comes from the constant air conditioners, swamp coolers and desert heat you are trapped in; then the water gets to you, the crappy, metallic-tasting liquid that makes you want to puke; and finally, the horrible air, the smog, the stink of it, and how it burns your eyes out. Like a victim of Nosferatu, the jungle infects you and you become a slave to it – and there is nothing better, no place on earth more addictive, compelling, necessary.

My first lesson with Sonny was anything but usual. I arrived at his place at the arranged time, knocked on the door, but there was no answer. Extremely nervous about meeting him, this only furthered my anxiety.

Suddenly a car pulled up – a Mercedes - and there he was. He got out of the car with a six pack of Coors and a pack of Camel cigarettes in hand. He walked over to me, smiled and said, "Hi boy," with the softest, warmest voice imaginable. A wave of kindness emanated from him, which surprised me.

Once inside his place, he immediately grabbed his alto off of his small living room table and proceeded to play a series of lightning-fast phrases that typified his brilliance and artistry. Then he asked me, "You wanna play like THAT, boy?" When I eagerly agreed, he said, "Good – just checkin'."

Then we sat down on his couch, and he stared at me, *hard.* No words were spoken for what seemed like forever and I felt extremely uncomfortable. Sonny had the most penetrating eyes imaginable and when he fixed them on you, it was impossible to turn away. Impossible.

After he stared and stared at me for what seemed like an eternity, he suddenly asked, "What's wrong with you, boy?"

Instantly, my brain went into a state of mad chaos. For six years I had held in a secret, a secret that had slowly and ruthlessly eaten away at me and destroyed me from within. But now, face to face with my idol, how could I lie to him? How could I hide the truth from him? HOW?

And so, I gave up. All those years of lying, hiding, acting - I couldn't do it anymore – not to Sonny. "My father killed himself when I was thirteen," I said, and broke down.

Sonny didn't say anything, but just nodded his head in some sort of recognition and confirmation. My darkest agony was now revealed to him, out in the open, for him to do with as he pleased, and I was suddenly terrified, terrified that he would laugh at me, tease me, reject me. But what did he do?

He loved me. He just loved me.

To hold in pain like that for so many years, from so many people, was beyond difficult. Sonny's insight had given me an incredible gift, the gift of for the first time since losing my father, *being honest*. For that and the freedom I suddenly felt in my heart, I owed him so much. At that exact moment in time, my love for him was born, love that would grow by leaps and bounds over the next eight months. To top it off, something else of major significance would occur between us, something that bound me even closer to him; an utterly simple thing, something from my past, something that I never thought in a million years would happen again.

20

As I had no wheels, I enlisted my best friend, Cooker, to drive me to my lessons with Sonny. As both of us were white, clueless and Canadian, we had no idea how dangerous it was for us to be in and around the black neighborhood where Sonny lived. Once there, Cooker would sit in his old, beat up, crappy-looking van, practicing paradiddles on his drum pad while waiting for my lesson to end. Though Cooker was a sitting duck, no one in the area ever bothered him, I'm sure because Sonny let everyone know that he was not to be touched. Sonny also made a point of coming out to greet Cooker after my lessons, giving him the "Sonny shake," a private handshake that Sonny only shared with the two of us — a tradition that Cooker and I carry on to this day, some forty-five spins later.

As my weekly lessons with Sonny began, I quickly realized that Sonny was not a formal teacher in any sense of the word. His lessons were mostly discussions about love, loyalty and commitment to music. He was also brutally honest; the most honest person I had ever met. Bullshit was not allowed in his presence, and he railed against it with everything he had. He wore his heart on his sleeve and always let me see what he was feeling. When he was up, the sun would burst into the room; but when he was down, his mood would turn the room into pure darkness. He was an extremely sensitive person, intuitive, and very private.

A few memories stand out from our time together. At one of our lessons, Sonny's new album, *The Joy Of Sax*, arrived in the mail. The album featured Sonny playing with a large ensemble of brass, winds and strings. Instantly, the lesson was over. Sonny put the record on and went into the kitchen to grab a beer. After we listened to only a few seconds of the first track, Sonny started laughing. When I asked him what was so funny, he said, "No matter how much they try to cover me up it's still me, boy! *It's still me!*" Then he ripped the album off of the turntable and gave it to me as a gift.

Sonny's loyalty towards music revealed itself during another lesson we shared. When I arrived, Sonny asked me what song I wanted to work on. When I replied, "Stella by Starlight," he asked me, "What are the words, boy?" When I hesitated, he asked again, "What are the words?" When I finally admitted to him that I didn't know them, he became enraged and yelled, "Pack up your horn – the lesson's over!" Even though I had just arrived, I packed up to leave, feeling totally humiliated. As I got to the front door, Sonny suddenly grabbed me by the arm, stared me down with anger in his eyes and shouted, "If you don't know the story, you don't know NOTHIN', boy!"

Suffice to say that from that moment forward, I learned the "story" of every song I played, to my great benefit.

At another lesson, I arrived at the usual time, knocked on the door, but received no answer. Suddenly a very large, scary-looking black dude who lived in the duplex above Sonny yelled down at me, "Hey, what the hell do you want?" When I told him I had a lesson with Sonny, he said, "What? He's not answering? Just a minute." Then he came racing down the stairs and started ferociously pounding on Sonny's door, yelling, "Wake up, Sonny! God dammit, wake up!" Finally, the door opened and there he was, the great Sonny Criss, in his pajamas and obviously very hungover. "What are you doing here, boy?" he asked quietly. When I told him we had a lesson, he paused for a moment and then said, "You're gonna pay, boy... scales." Then he went into the bathroom and with the door wide open took a long, noisy piss, followed by indulging in a power breakfast of a beer and a cigarette. Just another lesson with the master!

"They got me drunk for this, boy!"

21

After a few months of studying with Sonny, I decided to make a quick trip home to Vancouver. It was the summer of 1977, and I was nineteen years old. Once there, I found out my brother was playing a gig in town with his rock band, so I decided to go and surprise him. It was then that another mysterious, unexpected event occurred in my life, with someone I thought I would never see again.

A guitar player and singer, my brother was also a prolific songwriter and had written most of the songs for his band. As a performer he had a nice energy and charisma, but his career had never gotten off the ground the way he had hoped it would. Still, he kept at it, and I admired him for that.

As I headed up a long staircase to reach the top floor of the hall where he was performing, I suddenly saw a figure, face down, slumped over against the wall on one of the stairs. The person was concealed by a black jacket and appeared to be in distress. Having spent so much time with the homeless as a child, I couldn't just walk by without seeing if the person was okay, so I stopped and asked, "Hey, are you okay?"

After a brief moment, the figure suddenly moved and turned towards me, and when I saw her face I couldn't believe my eyes – *it was Tessa!* "Tessa?" I cried in disbelief. Upon hearing her name, she opened her eyes, looked at me and with an astonished look on her face answered, "Dylan?"

Instantly, we fell into each other's arms. To see each other again after ten years was overwhelming for both of us. For the first time, we kissed on the lips, over and over again, her touch transporting me to a place where angels lived. Despite the fact that she was in a bad way, she was tender and kind to me, and I fell in love with her all over again.

As we held and comforted each other, I apologized to her for not coming to her defense those many years before, but she just kept kissing me and whispering, "It's okay, it's okay, you're here now and I love you." Her beautiful response made all of the guilt I had carried for so long leave my mind and body, replaced by pure love and caring.

After a long time on the stairs, she said she really needed to go home to see her mother, and I got the feeling that she hadn't been home in quite some time. When I asked if I could come with her, she smiled and said her mother probably wouldn't understand, but that she would meet me tomorrow. True to Tessa and the way she had been since the first day we had met, she wanted us to be private from the world.

And so, I called a cab for her and sent her home. We exchanged phone numbers, and she asked me to call her that night. Then she gave me one more gorgeous kiss, thanked me and told me she loved me.

Too excited to go to my brother's performance, I went back to wherever I was crashing and called Tessa. We talked on the phone for a long time that night, dreaming of a future together, of having a family, of being together forever. When we finally said goodnight and I hit the pillow, I felt like I was sleeping on a cloud from the heavens.

But the next morning when I called her, she didn't answer. I tried again and again, but she didn't pick up. In those days there were no answering machines, so there was no way to leave a message for her. As I didn't know where her mother lived, I couldn't go to her either. I was stuck, unable to reach her. What had happened? Where was she? Why wouldn't she answer my calls?

And so, I lost Tessa all over again. I cried so hard over losing her. Although I knew she was suffering from a drug addiction which had landed her on those stairs in the first place, I thought I could help her and be there for her forever, but we never saw each other again.

Losing Tessa as a child was agonizing enough, but to lose her again ten years later was devastating. I cut my trip home short and escaped back to LA, where I hid in the Jungle from the searing pain that tore through my heart from losing her.

22

That fall, Sonny gave me the news that he was going to tour Japan to promote his new record. He was very excited about this, and when he got excited, his enthusiasm was infectious. It was great to see him so happy, and I was thrilled for him.

Just before Sonny was scheduled to leave for Japan, he secured a gig at The Lighthouse, a well-known jazz joint in Hermosa Beach, where he had played throughout his career. As I had never heard him play live before, I was more than pumped to go and see him there.

Once I arrived, I saw Sonny sitting with a woman, having a drink. As soon as he saw me, he got up, came over to me, and for the first time ever, hugged me.

Suddenly, wrapped in Sonny's embrace, a strange sensation came over me, a sensation I had not felt in a long time... it was my father! *It was my father hugging me!*

To feel that exact same feeling, the feeling I had been missing for so long, that I thought I would never experience again – it was incredible beyond description. I felt transported, lifted off the ground, floating somewhere; somewhere warm and so beautiful.

Chills ran up and down my spine as I tried to make sense of it. How could it be? How could he feel exactly the same as my father? Was I dreaming? Was this all just a fantasy?

As he held me in his arms for what seemed like an eternity, walls inside of me instantly disintegrated, crumbling into nothingness. Doors that had been closed, doors I didn't even know had existed, suddenly opened. My heart burst alive, sending love radiating through my entire being, as an avalanche of emotion overwhelmed me. I couldn't believe it. I simply couldn't believe it!

To feel what I felt at that moment, after so many lonely years, was a turning point in my life. Love was born inside of me once again, and with it, a renewed sense of confidence and belonging. All of this was a gift to me from Sonny - *all of it.*

How is it even possible to measure what he gave me that night? *How?*

23

As my old self was reborn, I became whole again, full of hopes and dreams. For the first time in six years, I walked around with a smile on my face. Happiness surrounded me, as the sun felt warmer, the roses prettier. Life showed me its beautiful side, and for the first time in a long time, I wanted to see it. And then there was my love, my sudden love, for Sonny. It was the same love, the exact same love that I had felt for my father all those years ago. As my love for Sonny blossomed, we shared many more beautiful hugs, and each time he held me, I felt my father. To say that this put me on cloud nine does not do justice to how I was feeling – it was more like cloud 999! So beautiful.

Just a few weeks after the gig at the Lighthouse, Sonny received a package in the mail from a woman from Paris that he obviously cared for. He showed me his excitement at receiving the package, turned his back on me to open it, but when he turned back around, the look on his face was one of utter sadness, pain, and heartbreak. Obviously, it was not what he had hoped for, and I never forgot the tortured look on his face that he showed me that day.

A few nights later, I accompanied Cooker to Redondo Beach, where his girlfriend lived. While they hung out at her apartment, I headed down to the beach with my alto. A far cry from the earlier days of playing in a room at school, Redondo was an unbelievably gorgeous spot, and as I stood there alone, facing the ocean and the sunset, I played my heart out.

Suddenly, I heard a crescendo of footsteps rush up behind me. I turned around, frightened, but no one was there. An eerie, ominous feeling surrounded me.

The next morning, a friend called and asked if I'd read the paper yet. When I said I hadn't, she blurted out, "Sonny's dead – he shot himself."

Instantly, I dropped the phone from my hand. Not Sonny! Not suicide! *Not again!*

Everything that was beautiful immediately flipped to evil; Buddha to Mara. My heart slammed shut. Doors closed. Hate and the devil regained their hold on me. I felt alone, so alone.

But something even more sinister suddenly made its presence known.

It was the voice again. But this time, it wasn't giving me an order or a command to follow. This time, it was making an observation.

It said, "The only common denominator between your father and Sonny is *you – it's your fault they killed themselves.*"

And, like a fool, I believed it.

24

In Shel Silverstein's brilliant book Different Dances, he describes "The Suicide Bullet." After a man shoots himself in the head, the bullet then goes through his wife, his child and out the other side. This is the legacy of suicide, and for me, it was no different.

The guilt that the voice had now planted inside of me began to crush me. I found it exceedingly difficult to get up every day and carry on with life. For what reason? What purpose? It was my fault that the two most important people in my life had died. Why should I deserve to live?

25

Now twenty years old, the aforementioned acne problem had become a full-blown nightmare. Hideous large boils covered my face and neck, forcing me to go to an acne clinic in desperation. Broke, lost and with zero confidence in myself, I sat in the waiting room with the other unfortunate customers. As we sat there in the city of angels, of beautiful people, of Hollywood starlets, we shared an agony; an agony of worthlessness, of ugliness, of wanting to hide from the world and remove ourselves from everyone in it. All I wanted to do was die and end my pathetic existence.

A broken person sees no light in the sunshine, only darkness. All the counselling, therapy, self-help books and quotes don't do anything when you are in this state, because you can't see or think straight; you are fucked, completely fucked, and are unable to find any solutions. This is what depression is and what I went through, full throttle, at this time of my life.

Feeling this way also made me hate the people around me who were happy. It wasn't their fault, I know, but their happiness spat in my face, over and over again, continuously reminding me of how fucked up I was, of what a loser I was, of how I was going nowhere.

There is a darkness beyond blackness that invades you during times like these. It takes hold of you and like a black hole, sucks the light out of your being. I was consumed by this darkness after my father's death, but now it became more than twice as dark after losing Sonny. As Beethoven concluded hundreds of years previously, no evil is more destructive than guilt, more destroying, more murdering from within; and the guilt that now controlled my existence utterly ravaged me and took me over.

It was under these nightmarish circumstances that a remembrance led me to a room, and to a man.

26

Approximately six months into the road gig with Perdido, we decided to add a trombone player to the band, mostly because of his expertise as an arranger. During one of our breaks from touring, he went down to LA and came back raving about a music school there. He urged us to think seriously about attending it, and so when I arrived in LA to study with Sonny, I took his advice and signed up at the school.

The Dick Grove Music Workshop school was exactly that – a non-accredited school where the top professional players, writers and arrangers in LA taught during their off-hours. It was a brilliant idea for a school, and not only did Dick run the place, but he also taught a one-year arranging program that, due to its solid reputation and success rate, attracted students from all over the world.

When we arrived in 1977, we were the first Canadians to attend the school, and Dick was more than excited to have us aboard. He and his staff went out of their way to make us welcome and be helpful to us, basically treating us like royalty.

Dick was an intriguing character, to say the least. He was a top-notch piano player, arranger and composer, and he seemed to know everybody in the LA music scene. His pet project, however, was his school and he poured himself into making it a great place, fueled by his enthusiasm, creative drive, and wicked sense of humour.

While I didn't have any classes with him in particular, I do remember him saying to all of us, "If you ever need to talk to me about something, anything, my door is always open." Many people offer things like this in life, but few really mean it. However, with Dick it felt different as there was a sincerity in his voice that rang true and registered with me.

And now, that sincerity was about to be put to the test.

Dick Grove

27

I was more than slightly nervous when I made my way upstairs to Dick's office. I have no recollection of how I remembered what he had offered, nor do I recall what day it was. All I do remember was that in one instant, I felt like I was nowhere, lost, in some sort of fucked-up fog, where I couldn't see or feel a thing; but in the next moment, I was suddenly outside of Dick's office knocking on his door.

True to his word, Dick welcomed me into his room and gave me his full attention. I sat down and before I knew it, out it came. Sonny had killed himself and I didn't know what to do. Then I started crying, trying to hold back the tears.

Dick sat there, staring at me. Despite the razor-sharp criticisms and cutting humour he oftentimes aimed at his students, Dick really cared about people – you could just sense it. He had a softness about him that was hidden most of the time, but today it revealed itself. He looked at me with kindness and empathy and then said something that changed my life forever. He said, "Why don't you try our man downstairs?"

That "man downstairs" was Philip H. Sobel.

Philip H. Sobel

28

At that time, it was virtually impossible to get a lesson from Phil. Students flew across the country from New York or drove down from San Francisco for the chance to take even a single lesson with him. But, thanks to Dick, a lesson was arranged, and before I knew it, I found myself in Phil's room for the first time. To say that I am indebted to Dick for making this happen is the greatest understatement of all time.

Philip H. Sobel, known to everyone as Phil, was a top-notch studio musician who played lead alto for the NBC Orchestra for eighteen years, along with doing countless studio sessions with the top musicians of the time, including Frank Sinatra, Ray Charles, and Luciano Pavarotti. But more than that, Phil was a gifted teacher. After studying with Henry Lindeman in New York, Phil worked for decades on expanding and refining Lindeman's brilliant ideas, while synthesizing them with several of his own amazing insights. Under his tutelage, he produced dozens of outstanding musicians who went on to have successful careers of their own, who owed any and all of their success to Phil's genius as a teacher.

I remember my first lesson with Phil like it was yesterday. I walked into his room, he put a piece of music on the music stand and said, "Play." After I played the first phrase (of four notes) he abruptly stopped me. "Do it again," he ordered, "but this time, pick your finger up slower." When I did as he requested, I heard a strange sound in my alto combined with an odd sensation in my finger. Startled, I abruptly stopped playing. Then Phil barked, "Tuesday at ten," and walked out of the room, slamming the door behind him.

What followed was eight years of the most intense training imaginable. The complete opposite of Sonny, Phil was unemotional, tough as nails, had a massive ego, and an "It's my way or the highway" approach. Phil pushed me hard, harder than anyone had ever pushed me before. He demanded my best at all times and had no qualms about letting me know when my playing wasn't up to his standards. Initially, I feared him, but I soon realized that underneath his rough, military-like exterior was a man driven to turn me into the best saxophone player possible. His lessons were so insightful and full of information that I started recording them so as to not miss any of the light of his genius. To this day, some forty-four years later, I am *still learning from those lessons*. Phil was an outstanding teacher in every sense of the word, and his dedication to me was second to none, which he proved on countless occasions.

An example of that dedication occurred when Phil's wife suddenly became ill. As my lesson with him was first thing in the morning, Phil would often arrive late, having been up all night with his wife. Barely able to function and his voice reduced to a whisper, he never felt sorry for himself and would instead apologize for being late. During this agonizingly difficult time for Phil, my one-hour lesson would oftentimes be reduced to twenty minutes or so, but two things stand out in my memory: he never cancelled a lesson with me, *not even once,* and those twenty minutes were worth more than it is possible to describe on the written page.

As soon as I started studying with Phil, he told me to quit all playing jobs so I could focus solely on my training. After a while, I ran out of money. Phil's solution? "Borrow from everyone you can." A short time later, I told him there was no one left to borrow from. His response? "Start adding up the lessons." While this arrangement made me very uncomfortable, I did as he demanded, and after a while, the lesson money I owed him added up to over $2,000.

Hanukah was around the corner, so I decided to give Phil a gift. I made a copy of our lessons I had transcribed and wrapped them in aluminum foil (as I had no money for wrapping paper). When I presented them to Phil he asked, "What's this?" After he opened it, he became quite emotional, which I had never seen before, and then he said, "Okay, Dyl, I've got a present for you, too – you don't owe me a penny for lessons... now PLAY."

A final example of his dedication to me occurred when, all of a sudden, something inside of me forced me to tell Phil of my father and Sonny's suicides. To say I was reluctant to do so is a gross understatement; in fact, I was terrified. The night before my lesson, I was beside myself with fear, and once the morning arrived, I became even more upset. As usual, Phil was late, which only served to compound my anxiety. When he finally did show up, I told him I had to tell him something and somehow got the words out. Then, I broke down in front of him.

Phil paused for a moment, and then said, "Look kid, I'm not going to kill myself, I'm not going anywhere, and if I do, I'll send you a plane ticket – now PLAY."

No greater words could have been spoken – it was exactly what I needed to hear and gave me not only a feeling of confidence, but that

I mattered to him. It was a turning point in our relationship, although we never spoke about it again.

Phil used to always tell me, "One day you're going to be the best alto player in this town." While that seemed not only improbable, but impossible, his faith in me pushed me to keep trying, to stay disciplined, to sacrifice everything to try and achieve this goal, a goal that we shared together. To have someone who believed in me that strongly gave me some of my confidence back, although it took years for me to become a whole person again.

What I realized years later was that Phil was actually a carbon copy of Coach Crosby, in his toughness, his demeanor and his expert knowledge of his craft. But there was one major difference between the two of them, one that separated them from each other, and that difference was this: *Phil didn't quit on me.*

He could've – but he didn't. He took me on, and he stuck it out with me for eight long years. For his efforts he received little compensation, but that seemed irrelevant to him. What really mattered, the point he was making, the most important lesson he taught me, was that in order to be successful, you have to go all in – *you have to give everything you've got* – otherwise you will fail.

My father had quit on me – so had Crosby - but not Phil - *not Phil.* And because of that, he was much more to me than just a saxophone teacher. He was a lifesaver, *my lifesaver,* plain and simple. He rebuilt me from the ground up and it was hard, difficult work. Most people would've never stuck with me as long as he did, and I owe him so much for that. In reality, I owe him the happiness I have today – how is it possible to put a price on that?

After eight enlightened years in his presence, I made the difficult decision to leave him and move back home. I remember talking with Phil about it, feeling distraught and upset about leaving, but then he said something that stuck with me. He said, "Go – even if things don't work out and you wind up back here, you'll be more than twice the man you are now." And so, I moved back to Canada to begin my recording and teaching career.

Over the next two decades, Phil and I stayed close and kept in regular contact until his death in 2008. He was one of a kind, a man with extremely high standards, a brilliant thinker and teacher. He taught me the saxophone, yes, but he also taught me about life, people, and the psychology of teaching.

Phil told me once, "Listen kid, I never had any talent for music, but what I had was stick-to-itiveness. I never gave up, so don't you either." That dedication he had, that inner drive that pushed him to never quit, was what pulled me out from under myself, what inspired me, what gave me a shot to start all over again.

Damn, I was fortunate to meet that man.

29

Fast forward fifteen spins – I'm back in Vancouver, married with two beautiful children, my career as a performer and teacher established, living a life of beauty and meaning. I've just turned forty-one, which is the same age my father was when he died. I feel like I'm on top of the world – but hold on a second; hold on; not so fast.

Josh Platzer was a bright, energetic, fun-loving, charismatic fifteen-year-old student of mine who I adored. He had a smile that was truly infectious, a fantastic sense of humour and a kindness that went beyond his tender age. While he did not possess any special musical talents, our lessons were ones I always looked forward to. While I made it a point in my private teaching to try and never play favorites, it was impossible not to feel a little something extra for Josh. He just had that "*it*" factor that, while indescribable, was both compelling and magnetic.

Unfortunately, there was another side to Josh, and slowly, over time, he revealed it to me. He told me he hated school and the bullshit teachers that he had to deal with. "They're nothing like you," he told me. He said he would often get so depressed about being there that he wouldn't attend class, but would instead sit outside the classroom by himself, happy in his own skin.

For the most part, I listened and tried to be a friend. I chalked up most of what he was feeling to teenager blues, which so many of my students suffered from. And because I was so happy and in such a good place for the first time in so long, I didn't pay enough attention. *I didn't pay enough attention!*

A few months into our time together, Josh told me he wanted to leave home. "I want to take a bus to San Francisco and live with the homeless people," he said. "It's my dream."

I thought that this was a very strange dream, especially for someone who was only fifteen, but I supported him and talked with him about it. Then he told me his parents wouldn't let him have a television in his room (which really pissed him off) and that they had put him on medication to try and help with his depression. Again, I listened and tried to support him as best as I could.

A few weeks later, he told me his parents had rejected his idea to go to San Francisco. He was very upset about this rejection, but his parents saying no didn't surprise me in the least – after all, it was a pretty outlandish dream to begin with. As I talked with him about it, I found myself thinking, *"If only Josh had my father, he could've done what he wanted."*

Summer came and our lessons were put on hold. Suddenly, Josh called and asked if we could go out for dinner. I was excited about this, as I hadn't seen him in a while. We met at a restaurant near my studio and had a great time together. He was so happy, energetic, and beautiful, and I felt a great sense of relief that he seemed so much better.

That's when he told me something that I should've listened to with more attention. He said, "When I take the medicine, it makes me feel better, so then I don't want to take it, and when I don't take it, that's when I go down, and when I go down, I can't control myself." After hearing that, I tried to encourage him to keep on the medication, that feeling good was the most important thing, and that hopefully, one day down the road, he would be able to stop taking it. I drove him home and we made plans to meet again and soon.

A few days later, I got a phone call from a student who was a friend of Josh's. When I answered he asked, "Are you sitting down?" In all my years, I had never heard anyone ask that question, and it hit me instantly that something was wrong, terribly wrong. And so, I sat down on the edge of the bed and nervously answered, "Yes?"

"Josh killed himself this morning," my student said. "He hung himself."

Sunday Sept 6th, 1998

Dear Dylan,

I'm sorry I didn't talk to you before, but I had to figure out what I was going to do first. I have come to realize that I was wasting your time with my lack of commitment to playing my saxaphone and I don't know where I will be with any form of commitment, to anything this year and I respect you too much to go on wasting your time. If its allright with you I would still like to play when you have a cancellation and maybe some time in the future I can play on a regular basis again. If you would like maybe we could meet every once in a while for a burger and talk. You have taught me to view life in a different way and you helped me through so many of my problems and you always have somthing intresting to tell me.

I'll hope to see you some time soon.

Josh Platzer

30

Like my father and Sonny's suicides, Josh's death was a complete surprise and shock. I found out later that his close friends knew about his plans and that they knew it was only a matter of time before he took his life, so if it's possible to be lucky in this kind of situation, they were most definitely the lucky ones. However, I wouldn't use the word "lucky" to describe how any of us felt that morning, and for the days that followed this excruciating nightmare.

As soon as I heard the news about Josh's suicide, my heart shattered all over again. I cried my eyes out for hours. He was such a beautiful kid, and this was so wrong. How could life be so cruel to take him? Why? *Why?*

Josh was so much like my father and Sonny. When he was up and feeling good, he illuminated everyone around him, but when he was down, shit – he fell hard. All three of them were like that, so vulnerable to life and its ups and downs.

But despite the pain that Josh's death brought, it also brought something else – it brought people together, and some of the people who came my way surprised me.

One of them was a kid from a large family. He had been a saxophone student of mine for about a year, and although not close to Josh, knew him and shared some of the same friends. At Josh's memorial service, he suddenly came over to me, put his arm around me and said, "I want you to know I'm here for you – if there's anything you need, just let me know, okay?" And then he gave me a huge hug accompanied by the most beautiful smile I had ever seen. How could he be so kind, so caring? At age fifteen? With no death experience? How?

A few months later, I was walking near my teaching studio and as I crossed the street, all of a sudden, a car blasted its horn right in front of me. Startled and pissed off, I stopped and angrily turned to face the driver – but then, I realized it was that kid. He had that same smile on his face, and as we waved to each other, we shared a beautiful, private moment together.

Two brothers who took lessons from me were also extraordinarily kind to me during this nightmare. One of them had made the phone call to tell me about Josh, and I'd often thought about how hard that must've been for him. After Josh died, both of them were unbelievably kind and supportive to me, and for some reason, went out of their way to do so. They put their own feelings and pain aside to care for me – again, so young, with no experience – how? Why? *Why me?*

At the memorial service for Josh, I was asked to start it off by playing my saxophone, which was gut-wrenching in the extreme. The entire service was enveloped by people crying, most of them Josh's friends, and was the saddest funeral I had ever been to. Afterwards, an informal gathering was held at Josh's home. Arriving late, I made my way through and around the many people there, when suddenly, Josh's eleven-year-old sister saw me, motioned me over to the couch where she was sitting and grabbed onto me. No words were spoken as I felt a strange nervousness engulf me. After a while, her father tried to pull her away from me to comfort her himself, but she refused and held on even tighter. Somehow, she knew that I was an expert at this kind of thing – somehow, she knew.

Josh's suicide ripped me apart and produced the inevitable feelings of guilt inside me, yet again. If I had listened more carefully, maybe I could've saved him – but I didn't. I was too damn happy in my own skin to pay attention. Afterwards, I hated myself for that happiness.

31

Just before my father died, he was interviewed on a local television show, ironically at the same station he had worked for years earlier. I was in the audience as he was questioned about his life and change from straight to communal, along with his work at The *Georgia Straight and with the homeless. I forgot about this show for years after his death, until one day, out of the blue, it popped into my mind.*

In 1980, while living in LA and studying with Phil, I met two people who would become my best friends for life. W.G. Horrocks and C.H. Powell were the two most incredible souls I had ever met, and the three of us hit it off instantly. Our personalities connected flawlessly, and our friendship was rooted in creative endeavours, intellectual discussions and a ton of laughter. Though we shared a house together for only three years, we remained best friends for the rest of our lives.

It was during that time together that I suddenly remembered my father's television interview. When I told C.H. about it, he was fascinated and wanted to see it. Being in the tv business himself, he started making some calls. While the show had been filmed in Vancouver, he discovered that Dick Clark Productions, an LA company, had produced it. As they had an office in Burbank, a stone's throw from where we lived in East Hollywood, C.H. inquired about the possibility of getting his hands on a copy.

As the show had been taped in 1971, nine years earlier, the Production company informed C.H. that most likely there would not be a copy available. Disappointed, I thanked C.H. for his efforts and forgot about it.

But to my astonishment, the very next day, they called C.H. to tell him they had found a copy! Immediately, he paid to have a video tape of it made, and just a day later, we had a copy of the interview ready to go into our VCR!

As the three of us sat down in front of the tv, I was beside myself. Ever since my father had died, I had forgotten his voice. The nightmares of him speaking to me with no sound had diminished, but now, almost ten years later, he was about to walk out onto the stage and speak. I couldn't believe I was going to see and hear him again.

Suddenly, the show came on and there he was. As soon as he spoke, the sound of his voice instantly registered in me. I burst into tears and hugged my friends. It was one of the most incredible moments of my life. He was there, alive, my father!

The experience of "meeting" my father again was a huge factor in my healing process, a process that took decades, and to have my best friends there with me made it all the more special.

What also stayed with me from this event was the mysteriousness of it. What were the chances that the show was sitting in a vault, just a few miles away, so close to where I was living? And how did they find a copy of it so quickly? It was mind-boggling to say the least, almost as if someone had arranged for it to happen. Had someone? A spirit guide, perhaps?

Many people have stated that everything in life is preordained. Religious types have maintained that "God" controls all things, while others have rationalized life and its scenarios by the phrase, "Everything happens for a reason."

I don't know what the correct answer is as to why things happen, or if there is just one answer, or perhaps many. Maybe Bob Dylan had it right when he wrote, "The answer is blowin' in the wind." I don't know. But what I *do* know is this: that over and over during my lifetime, mysterious things have happened in and around me, things I can't explain or make sense of. And so, I have learned to accept them, along with the fact that for as long as I am here, there will be more of them headed my way. Somehow, there is a comfort in this knowledge.

32

You don't measure a person by how much money they make – you measure them by how many people they touch. Society has it all wrong, all backwards. Yes, I know you have to have money to survive, but you have to have love too, don't you? You have to care about people and do all you can to help them, don't you? Don't you? Or are you just here to serve yourself?

My father truly cared about people, too much so - that was his crime. He tried to help, to make a difference, to *really make a difference,* but in the end, he gave up and quit on himself and the rest of us.

What happened to him? Why did he end his life? Why did he leave me?

From what I've been able to surmise over all of these years, everything started with frustration. Stuck in the straight world, trapped in married life, living a non-creative existence, the peace/anti-war movement of the sixties offered him a way out. But out of that decision to change his lifestyle, to become involved with the movement, another deeper passion was born in my father - to help people less fortunate than him.

In a letter he sent to us shortly before he died he wrote, "Like a Jew surviving the Holocaust, I offer a refinement of myself. I am going to dedicate the rest of my life to helping the homeless, the downtrodden, the less fortunate." And so, for the short time he was here, he did just that.

How do I know this? Over the fifty years since his death, I have met countless people who have told me so. They have made a point to find me, to let me know how my father helped them, rescued them off the streets and cared for them when no one else gave a damn.

Most of us throw a few coins at the homeless to make us feel better; others do nothing, while some of us even scowl at them like they're subhuman, unworthy of our attention, but my father wasn't like any of those types. He couldn't be involved with the homeless peripherally. He had to immerse himself and go *all in.* He just had to.

In this way, he taught me the same lesson Phil did - that, in order to accomplish anything, you have to have total dedication and determination – you have to give everything you've got to conquer whatever it is you're trying to achieve. The history of the greats corroborates this. Unfortunately, my father paid a heavy price for this commitment – he lost everything, everyone, and then himself.

Just before he died, he told me of his dream - to open a shelter where the homeless could come in, get a bath, a shower and shave, some food, warm clothing and a place to crash. I remember thinking how beautiful his dream was and I noticed how his eyes lit up when he talked about it.

Unfortunately, it never came to fruition, but something else did: my father became extremely lonely.

Away from his wife and family for a few years, he suddenly appeared at the commune one day and suggested that my mother move out, so he could move back in. My mother was surprised by his sudden request and hesitated to answer, but my brother and sister resisted the idea, so it was dropped.

Feeling alone and rejected, my father left, a beaten man.

A few nights later, he got a hose from the garage where he was living, attached it to the exhaust pipe of his car, turned the car on, got into the back seat and said goodbye to the world. By the time I got home from school the next day, he had already been cremated.

At the time, I didn't know he had tried to kill himself before. When he was nineteen, he tried to smother himself with a pillow because, like a lot of Jews after the Holocaust, he felt guilty he was spared, while so many other innocent people weren't. That damn guilt that Beethoven talked about, raising its ugly head yet again.

Another time, he downed a bunch of pills one afternoon at work. My sister told me years later that he had done it to try and get my mother's attention, but it didn't work and instead just pissed her off. Apparently, when my sister asked my mom what to do about him, she said, "Just leave him on the floor."

But finally, he got what he wanted. And in a sad irony, he killed himself on Census Day. The government's catch phrase for the census that year was "Count Me In." When my father's friend arrived home to find him, he also found a note that read: "Count Me Out." One last joke on the way out...

Something that has bothered me for the past fifty years since he died: why didn't he tell me he was hurting? Why didn't he let me know he was in pain? If I was so special to him, such a vital part of his life, why didn't he give me a chance to try and help him? I know I was just a child, but maybe if he had told me he was suffering, I might've said something childlike in response that could've turned his thinking around. Something like, "Why don't we take off and go on a trip together?" Or, "How about I move in with you?" *Why didn't he even give me a chance?*

But instead of doing so, he kept his feelings, his dark feelings, secret from me. He never let me see him with his guard down, *not even once during our entire time together*. Perhaps he was protecting me, along with protecting the beauty of our relationship, not wanting to inject any unhappiness or conflict into it. Although I understand and accept that, I still wish he would've given me a chance to help him - just one chance. But he never did, and my heart aches with pain because of it.

Of course, I understand and accept the argument that one should not tell a child such things. How could it possibly be of benefit for a kid of thirteen to know that his father was thinking of killing himself? How could it not do damage down the road? I get all this, I get it, but I still wish he would've given me the chance. *Just one chance.*

I don't want to be angry at my father, but sometimes it's impossible not to be. He destroyed my life. When you invest everything in one person and then they quit on you, it crushes you, mutilates your spirit and leaves you scarred for the duration. That's what he did to me. He might not have quit on me on purpose, but his suicide sent that message loud and clear and it hurt like hell. I mean, we missed so much. We never got to hang out as adults. We never got to talk about women. Not even one intellectual discussion between us – not even one.

Still, I love him and respect him for what he tried to accomplish. Anyone who gives everything they've got to try and help, to try and make a difference, is worthy of respect. My father sacrificed *everything*—his family, his comforts, his reputation, and then finally, his life to try and help people. How many of us do that? How many of us give everything we've got? Not many.

When you love someone as much as I loved my father and then you lose them, you never fully recover. You are destined to be chained to them and to search for that love for the rest of your life. Even now, five decades later, I am still searching. It is a lonely, painful search and I don't think I will ever find that love again.

And so it is in this duality that I live when I think of him. Hate beside love; anger mixed with respect; brutal pain with a remembrance of happiness. Buddha and Mara. This is what he left me as I chase him, trying to catch up to him, to be even half the man he was to this world.

I have tried to make it a worthy chase.

Muhammad Ali said, "I'm gonna win my title back, then walk down the alleys and help my brothers and sisters." He and my father were the same in this way. Both of them picked up strangers, brought them home, fed them, gave them a place to sleep. Both of them helped people less fortunate than themselves, without asking for anything in return – true, honest charity, something that has almost disappeared from today's world. It makes me so proud to know my father was like Ali in this way. We need more like them - so many more. There is never enough love, kindness, caring never enough. I mean, how could there be?

EPILOGUE

Now sixty-four, I've survived four months since I morphed into The Terminator. The heart doc has just given me the news that I have a genetic disorder called "Bicuspid Aortic Valve Disease," another fancy term medical people throw around like Marino throwing a bomb to Clayton or Duper. And what does it mean? It means I've got two heart flaps to move my blood around instead of the usual three, and because of this, my heart is not getting as much blood to my aorta as it needs. How bloody ironic! After all the crap I've had to endure, I should have FOUR flaps, not two!

Life is painful. We all get dragged through it, some of us more so than others, but no one makes it through unscathed. Even if your life goes perfectly, you die. No one escapes this place untouched. Everyone gets burned.

My father used a hose; Sonny, a gun; Josh, a rope. For them, ending their life was a solution to the pain they had to endure. When you break your arm, you go to the hospital, and they set it in a cast. But what do you do when your mind is broken? Or your heart? *How do you repair those?*

And what about the ones who are left behind? *How are we supposed to cope?* For me personally, my fate has been to be stuck carrying a deep insecurity everywhere I go. Because of this, when I meet someone that touches my heart, I fall too quickly. I latch on too fast, way too fast, exerting undue pressure on them to do the same. Then I tell them I love them, again before I should, which only serves to upset and confuse them even more (Why is the word "love" such a difficult word for people to hear?). Most of the time, their reaction is to get rid of me, oftentimes attacking me, insinuating that I did something wrong, by caring about them too much and too soon (Really? Caring too much?). This pattern, born from my need to replace the love I have lost and the rejection I feel, has repeated itself over and over in my life, and I can't seem to control it or manage it at all, and every time it happens, I hate it and myself.

Why do I do this? Why do I make people that I supposedly care for so uncomfortable, so soon after I meet them? Why do I grab on so quickly, with such desperation? Because, as Josephine Hart so brilliantly wrote in her masterpiece *Damage, I am damaged*. I am fucked up by the suicides I have experienced. When my father, Sonny, and Josh killed themselves, they created a hole in me that I have spent my entire life trying to fill, unfortunately, without success. As I try to replace the love I felt for them, desperately so, I try too hard, and then I scare people and drive them away, which sends me right back to square one all over again – alone and lonely. I'm not proud of my behaviour, but in some way, it reveals my character and who I am as a person, and as Oscar Wilde so brilliantly observed, "But then one regrets the loss of even one's worst habits. Perhaps one regrets them the most. After all, they are such an essential part of one's personality."

So, unless you know me, *really know me*, you won't be able to accept or understand this messed-up part of who I am. There have been some, very few, who have stuck by me over the years, but not many. Somehow, with their incredible kindness and maturity, they have been able to love and care enough to accept me for who I am, *faults included.* To them, I owe so much, for they have kept me here, kept me believing in myself, kept me trying.

We need more people like this on earth. We need to be more compassionate, more understanding, more caring. We judge people way too fast, before we really know what's going on with them. Then we act surprised when they do something unexpected. We need to pay closer attention. We need to care more and try harder.

We need to try harder.

I still have hope. I still believe in people, in love. I still think we can improve, love each other better, try harder to be there for each other. As John Lennon sang, "All you need is love." I'm not sure if that's all we need, but it's a damn good start.

In the television interview my father did, he said that a revolution starts by getting out onto the streets and getting to know the people. Then, one by one, we can start to change people's thinking. So, here's an idea: today, right now, go out into the world and spend some time with someone in need. Comfort them, show kindness. Help in any way you can. We have to start somewhere.

ONE MORE MYSTERIOSO

Fifty-five years since the peace movement began and we're still at war. What the fuck is the matter with us? I'll tell you what's the matter with us – we're flawed. Our DNA is screwed up. We'd rather spend our time fighting and killing each other than living together peacefully. What a screwed-up race we are. We should be ashamed of ourselves.

In 1997, when I was thirty-nine years old, on my way from Vancouver to Montreal to sign my first recording contract, I suddenly ran into someone totally unexpected – my father.

As I stepped off the top stair of the escalator, there he was, seated alone, with no bags, just staring at me. There was no mistaking it was him, despite the fact that he'd been dead for twenty-six years.

As I tried to make sense of his presence, we both seemed to be stuck in some sort of time warp. What was going on? Was I hallucinating? How could that be him*? How could he just be sitting there?*

When I tried to open my mouth to speak, it wouldn't move, just like when I had been on the bus with Tessa. All I could do was stare at him, as if in some sort of trance.

Finally, after what seemed like eons of time, the logical part of my brain took over. "That can't be him" it said. "There's no way that's him. Stop being so foolish. Move on... move on."

And so, I did.

But after only a few steps, my heart took over. It cried out, "Don't leave him! Go back to him! Go back!"

And so, I turned around, excited, but he was gone – vanished. And then, my heart burst into a million pieces all over again…

After I got back from my trip, I went to see a friend who had been rescued off the street by my father years earlier. When I told her what had happened, she smiled and said, "Next time, talk to him."

Strangely, just two weeks later, she died of natural causes. Natural causes – really? Or did my father call on her to join him? I often wonder about that. Yet another unexplainable, mysterious event. But no matter what happened, I hope she's with him, they're laughing and having a good time; and that one day, he does come back to see me, because this time, *this time* – I'll be ready.